MONA

Or, The Secret of a Royal Mirror

MRS. GEORGIE SHELDON

1st WORLD
LIBRARY
Literary Society

Mona

Mrs. Georgie Sheldon

© 1st World Library, 2008
PO Box 2211
Fairfield, IA 52556
www.1stworldlibrary.com
First Edition

LCCN: 2007940228

Softcover ISBN: 978-1-4218-9337-2
Hardcover ISBN: 978-1-4218-9437-9
eBook ISBN: 978-1-4218-9237-5

Purchase *"Mona"*
as a traditional bound book at:
www.1stWorldLibrary.com/purchase.asp?ISBN=978-1-4218-9337-2

1st World Library is a literary, educational organization
dedicated to:

- Creating a free internet library of downloadable ebooks

- Hosting writing competitions and offering book publishing
scholarships.

Interested in more 1st World Library books? contact:
literacy@1stworldlibrary.com
Check us out at: www.1stworldlibrary.com

1ˢᵗ World Library Literary Society

Giving Back to the World

"If you want to work on the core problem, it's early school literacy."

- James Barksdale, former CEO of Netscape

"No skill is more crucial to the future of a child, or to a democratic and prosperous society, than literacy."

- Los Angeles Times

"Literacy... means far more than learning how to read and write... The aim is to transmit... knowledge and promote social participation."

- UNESCO

"Literacy is not a luxury, it is a right and a responsibility. If our world is to meet the challenges of the twenty-first century we must harness the energy and creativity of all our citizens."

- President Bill Clinton

"Parents should be encouraged to read to their children, and teachers should be equipped with all available techniques for teaching literacy, so the varying needs and capacities of individual kids can be taken into account."

- Hugh Mackay

CHAPTER I

A FASCINATING YOUNG WIDOW
OPENS THE STORY

"Appleton, don't look quite yet, but there's a woman just behind you whom I want you to see. I never before saw such a face and figure! They are simply perfection!"

The above remarks were made by a young man, perhaps thirty years of age, to his companion, who, evidently, was somewhat his senior.

The two gentlemen were seated at a private table in the dining-room of a large hotel in Chicago, Illinois, and were themselves both handsome and distinguished in appearance.

"There!" the speaker continued, as a slight commotion near them indicated that some one was rising from a table; "she is about to leave the room, and now is your chance."

The gentleman addressed turned to look as the lady passed; but the moment she was beyond the possibility of hearing he broke into a laugh of amusement.

"Oh, Cutler!" he exclaimed; "I never would have believed that you could rave so over a red-head—you who all your life have held such hair in detestation!"

"Well," returned Mr. Cutler, flushing guiltily, "I acknowledge that I have always had a peculiar aversion to red hair; but, truly, hers is an unusual shade—not a flaming, staring red, but deep and rich. I never saw anything just like it before. Anyhow, she is a magnificent, specimen of womanhood. See! what a queenly carriage! what a figure!" and his glance followed the lady referred to, lingeringly, admiringly.

"Yes, she certainly is a fine-looking woman," his companion admitted; "and, if I am any judge, the diamonds she wears are worth a small fortune. Did you notice them?"

"No; I saw only herself," was the preoccupied response.

"Aha! I see you are clean gone," was the laughing rejoinder of Mr. Appleton.

The lady referred to was indeed a strangely attractive person. She was rather above the medium height, straight as an arrow, with a perfectly molded figure, although it was somewhat inclined to *embonpoint*, while her bearing was wonderfully easy and graceful. Her complexion was exquisitely fair, her features round, yet clearly cut and regular. She had lovely eyes of blue, with a fringe of decided, yet not unbecoming red upon their white lids, while her hair was also a rich but striking red, and was worn short, and curled about; her fair forehead and down around her alabaster neck in bewitching natural rings.

She was apparently about twenty-five or twenty-eight years of age, with all the strength and *verve* of perfect health in her movements. She was dressed wholly in black, which served but to enhance her fairness, while in her ears and at her throat she wore peculiar ornaments shaped like small crescents, studded with diamonds, remarkable for their purity and brilliancy.

For several days Mr. Cutler and Mr. Appleton sat at the same table, and were quietly observant of this lovely woman.

She came and went, apparently unconscious of their notice or admiration, was gently dignified in her bearing and modest in her deportment, and the two gentlemen became more and more interested in her.

Upon inquiring, they learned that she was a young widow—a Mrs. Bently, whose husband had recently died very suddenly. He was supposed to have been very wealthy, but, there being no children, there was some trouble about the settlement of the property, and she was boarding in the city until matters should be adjusted, when she contemplated going abroad.

She seemed to be an entire stranger to every one, and very much alone, save for the companionship of a maid, by whom she was always attended, except at meal-time. Mr. Appleton was called from the city about ten days after his attention was first called to her, but his friend, Mr. Cutler, was still a guest at the hotel, and before the expiration of another week he had managed to make the acquaintance of the fascinating widow.

The more he saw of her the more deeply interested he became, until he began to realize that his interest was fast merging into a sentiment of a more tender nature.

Mr. Cutler was an energetic young broker, and report said that he was rapidly amassing a fortune, and ere long would be rated rich among rich men. He was fine-looking, very genial and social in his nature, and so, of course, was a general favorite wherever he went.

His admiration for Mrs. Bently soon became the subject of remark among his acquaintances at the hotel, and they predicted that the fair and wealthy widow would soon capture the gallant and successful broker.

Six weeks spent in the attractive widow's society convinced Justin Cutler that she was as lovely in character as in person. She was remarkably sweet-tempered, very devout, and charitable beyond degree. She would never listen to or indulge in gossip of any kind; on the contrary, she always had something kind and pleasant to say to every one.

Upon several occasions, Mr. Cutler invited her to attend the theatre, lectures and concerts, and she honored him by graciously accepting his attentions; while, occasionally, he was permitted to accompany her to church.

That faultless face, her unvarying amiability, her culture and wit, were fast weaving a spell about him, and he had decided to ask her to share his fate and fortune, when he suddenly missed her from her accustomed seat at the table, and failed to meet her about the house as usual.

For three days he did not see anything of her, and he began to be deeply troubled and anxious about her. He could not endure the suspense, and made inquiries for her. He was told that she was ill, and this, of course, did not relieve his anxiety.

On the fourth day, however, she made her appearance again at dinner, but looking so pale and sad, that his heart went out to her with deeper tenderness than ever.

He waited in one of the parlors until she came out from the

Mrs. Georgie Sheldon

dining-room. She made her appearance just as a lady, one of the hotel guests, was leaving the room. With eagerness he stepped forward to greet her, and then, with kind solicitude, inquired regarding her recent illness.

"Thank you, Mr. Cutler; I have not been really ill," she said, with a pathetic little quiver of her red lips, "but—I am in deep trouble; I have had bad news."

"I am very sorry," returned the young broker, in a tone of earnest sympathy. "Shall I be presuming if I inquire the nature of your ill-tidings?"

She smiled up at him gratefully.

"Oh, no, and you are very kind. It—it is only a business trouble," she said, a vivid flush dyeing her fair cheek; "but being a woman, perhaps I cannot meet it with quite the fortitude of a man."

"Can I help you in any way?" the gentleman asked, eagerly. "Come into the little reception-parlor yonder—there is no one there—and confide in me, if you will honor me so far."

The fair widow took the arm he offered her, and he led her within the room, and shut the door.

"Sit here," he said, placing a comfortable rocker for her, then he sat opposite her, and waited for her to open her heart to him.

"You know," she began, falteringly, "that I have lost my husband; he died several months ago, and there has been some trouble about the settlement of his estate.

"His relatives contested the will, but my lawyer has always

assured me that he could at least secure a handsome amount for me, even if he could not win the whole. But the first of this week, I learned that I am to have almost nothing—that there was not nearly as much as at first supposed, and Mr. Bently's relatives will get that: and so—I am penniless."

"Oh, not so badly off as that, I hope!" exclaimed Mr. Cutler, looking grave.

"It is true. My lawyer's charges will take every dollar that is coming to me, and—oh! it is humiliating to tell you of it—I owe a great deal of money here at this hotel, besides. I never dreamed," she went on, hurriedly, and flushing hotly again, "but that I could pay my bills. I thought that I should have a large fortune, and I—I am afraid that I have been very extravagant: but now—I do not know *what* I shall do."

Mr. Cutler saw that she was in a very perplexing situation, and she seemed so crushed by it that all his tenderest sympathies were enlisted.

"If you would allow me to lend you any amount," he began, when the widow showed him the first burst of temper that he had ever seen her exhibit.

"Sir, do you suppose I would *borrow* what I could never expect to pay?" she cried, with almost passionate scorn, and flushing to her temples.

"I beg your pardon," Justin Cutler returned, feeling almost as if he had been guilty of an inexcusable insult; "believe me, I would not wish to put you under any obligation that would be burdensome."

Then he asked himself if it would be safe for him to tell her of his love then and there, lay his fortune at her feet, and thus

Mrs. Georgie Sheldon

relieve her from her present trouble and all anxiety for the future.

But he feared she might resent the offer, coming at such a time—think it was prompted more by pity than affection, and reject it as scornfully as she had refused his offer of a loan.

She was very attractive as she sat there before him, her white hands folded on her lap, her eyes cast down in troubled thought, and a grieved expression about her beautiful mouth, and he longed, with all the earnestness of his generous nature, to help her in this emergency.

Suddenly his face lighted.

"Are you willing to confide in me the amount of your indebtedness, Mrs. Bently?" he gently asked.

She falteringly named a sum that staggered him, and told him that she had indeed been very extravagant.

"I—I have always had what I wanted. I have never had to count the cost of anything, for my husband was very generous and indulgent," she apologized, with evident embarrassment, as she met his grave look.

"May I make a practical suggestion without the fear of offending you?" the young man questioned, with some confusion.

"Oh, if you would!" cried his companion, eagerly, her face brightening, while she uttered a sigh of relief, as if she expected that his suggestion, whatever it might be, would lift the burden from her heart.

"You have some very costly jewels," Mr. Cutler remarked, the color deepening in his cheek as he glanced at the flashing stones in her ears; "perhaps you would be willing to dispose of them and thus relieve yourself from your present embarrassment."

"Oh, you mean sell my—my diamonds?" cried the lovely widow, with a little nervous sob, and instantly her two white hands went up to her ears, covering the blazing gems from his sight, while a painful flush leaped to her brow and lost itself beneath the soft rings of her burnished hair.

"Yes," pursued Mr. Cutler, wondering at her confusion. "If I am any judge, they are very valuable stones, and I suppose you might realize a handsome sum upon them."

He was secretly planning to redeem them and restore them to her later, if she should favorably regard his suit.

"But—but;" and her confusion became intensified a hundred-fold, "they aren't *real*. I'd be glad enough if they were, and would willingly sell them to cancel my indebtedness, but they are only *paste*, although an excellent imitation."

Her companion regarded her with astonishment.

"You surely do not mean that?" he exclaimed, "for if I ever saw pure white diamonds, those which you wear are certainly genuine."

"No, they are not," she returned, shaking her head with a positive air. "I am very fond of diamonds and I had some very nice ones once, but they were stolen from me just after my husband died. I could not afford to replace them, just then, and I had these made to wear until I could do so. They were made in Paris, where they are very clever at such work.

I hoped when my husband's estate was settled, I could have some real stones again; but, of course, I cannot *now*," she regretfully concluded.

"Will you allow me to examine them, please?" Mr. Cutler asked, still sure that the stones were genuine.

Mrs. Bently unhesitatingly removed one of the crescent ornaments from her ear and laid it in his hand.

He examined it critically and was still confident that it was really composed of precious gems. He believed that if she had had them made to order to replace the stolen ones, either the jeweler had been guilty of a wretched blunder, or else some friend had interposed to replace the jewels which she so regretted.

"I am sure there is some mistake. I am confident that these are real diamonds and very valuable," he asserted, positively.

"Oh, no, they are *not*," she repeated, with grave assurance.

Then she naively added, and with a little ripple of laughter:

"I am glad to know that they are so good an imitation as to deceive you. There is some comfort in that, although it is not pleasant to have to acknowledge the sham."

Still her companion was not convinced. Surely no paste jewels ever emitted such a brilliant white light as those which lay upon his palm, catching and reflecting the various colors about them in such dazzling gleams.

"Would you be willing to go with me to some reliable jeweler and have them tested?" he asked.

The lovely woman flushed crimson.

"No, I couldn't do that; I should not like to—to have it known that I had been wearing such things," she said. "To be sure," she added, with a quick upward glance that made her companion thrill with secret joy, "I have confessed it to you, but you were so kind and sympathetic I—I trusted you involuntarily."

"Thank you," Justin Cutler returned, a brilliant smile lighting his face, and he longed to open his heart to her, but deemed it better to wait a while. "Then, if you would not like to go with me, will you trust the stones with me, and allow me to have them tested for you?"

"Of course I will, if you want to take that trouble; though," she added, with a little skeptical laugh, as she removed the crescent from her other ear and gave it to him, "I assure you the trust isn't such a responsible one as you imagine."

"We shall see," he smilingly responded, as he put the ornaments carefully in his purse and arose, "I shall submit them to some reliable dealer in diamonds, get him to set a value upon them, and will inform you of the verdict this evening."

"Thank you, Mr. Cutler—you are very kind to be so interested for me," the beautiful woman gratefully murmured.

"I would I might," the young man began, eagerly, then suddenly checked himself and added, "might assist you in some way regarding your other troubles."

Again he had been on the point of declaring himself, but told himself that the moment was not a propitious one.

"I am afraid it is too late for that," she responded, with a sigh; "the case is settled, and Mr. Bently's relatives have won. But, good-by—do not let me detain you longer."

"I will see you again this evening," he returned, adding, as he passed out of the room: "I will be very careful of your property, and hope to bring you a good report."

Mrs. Bently shrugged her graceful shoulders indifferently, as if she had no faith in his belief, and felt that it would be but a small loss if the jewels were never returned. Then, with a smile and a bow, she went up stairs to her own rooms.

CHAPTER II

THE VICTIM OF A WOMAN'S WILES

Justin Cutler, after leaving the hotel, went directly to one of the first jewelers of the city, a well-known diamond expert, and submitted Mrs. Bently's ornaments to his judgment.

"They are remarkably fine stones." Mr. Arnold remarked, after having carefully examined them through a microscope; "very pure and clear, most of them without a flaw. So far as I can see, there is not one of them that is in the least off-color."

"I thought so," was Mr. Cutler's inward and exultant comment; but he simply asked, as if he accepted the man's verdict as a matter of course: "What is your estimate of their value?"

"Well," said the jeweler, smiling, "if you wish to know their real value just for your own satisfaction, I can give it; but that might considerably exceed the amount I should be willing to name in case you might wish to dispose of them to me."

"I understand," Mr. Cutler returned; "but what would they be worth to you—what would you be willing to give for the stones?"

Mr. Arnold considered the matter a few moments, and then named a sum which Mr. Cutler deemed a fair price under the circumstances, and one which he felt sure Mrs. Bently would be only too glad to secure in her emergency.

"You make that offer for them, then—you will purchase them if the lady agrees to take the sum you have named?" he asked.

"Yes, and the offer shall be open for her acceptance or refusal for three days.'

"Thank you; I will see you again before the time expires," Mr. Cutler replied; and, taking up the diamonds, which Mr. Arnold had placed in a small box, he put them carefully away in an inside pocket and left the store.

When he returned to his hotel he sent his card up to Mrs. Bently, with a request that she would see him for a few moments in the reception-room. But he was greatly disappointed when the waiter returned and said that the lady was out.

He had an engagement for the evening, and thus he would not be able to see her until the next morning. He was somewhat troubled, for he did not like to retain her diamonds over night; but since he could not return them to her, he judged they would be safer about his person than anywhere else, and so did not remove them from his pocket.

The next morning he was early in his place at breakfast-time and anxiously awaiting the appearance of Mrs. Bently.

She soon came in, looking much brighter and fresher than she had been the day before, and he noticed that she was in her traveling-dress.

Could she be contemplating leaving the hotel? he asked himself, with a sudden sense of depression.

She smiled and bowed as she passed him, and he remarked, in a low tone, as he returned her salutation:

"I will wait for you in the reception-room."

She nodded assent, but a gleam of amusement shot into her expressive eyes, which he interpreted to mean that she believed he had failed in his errand and would be obliged to acknowledge the truth of what she had told him about her ornaments.

This thought greatly elated him, and he chuckled to himself as he imagined her astonishment when he should inform her of the offer of the diamond merchant.

He soon finished his breakfast and repaired to the reception-room, where he drew forth his morning paper to while away the time until Mrs. Bently should appear.

But she did not hurry, and he began to grow impatient. Evidently she had no faith in the genuineness of the stones, and had no intention of spoiling her breakfast just to be told what she already knew.

It was nearly half an hour before she came to him, but he could forgive her for making him wait, for her greeting was unusually cordial, and she seemed lovelier than ever in her pretty dress of dark gray trimmed with black. It was made very high at the throat, and fitted her perfect form like a glove. Her face was like a flawless pearl, and he had begun to think the soft ruddy rings that crowned her milk-white brow and made her look so youthful, the most beautiful hair in the world.

Mrs. Georgie Sheldon

He sprang to his feet, his face all aglow, and went forward to take the hand she extended to him.

"I have such good news for you, Mrs. Bently," he said, as he drew the little box from his pocket. "Your gems are real after all," and he slipped them into her hand as he spoke.

She lifted a startled, incredulous look to his face.

"You cannot mean it—you are only jesting!" she cried.

"Indeed no; I would not jest and I do mean just what I have said," he persisted.

"Impossible! Why, Mr. Cutler, I gave less than ten dollars for the crescents."

The young man looked blank.

"Then some one has made an expensive blunder, and set real diamonds for you instead of paste. Where did you purchase them—or order them made?"

"Of Hardowin & Leroux, under the Palais Royal, Paris, less than a year ago," Mrs. Bently promptly responded.

"It does not seem possible that any one could have made such a costly mistake," Justin Cutler said, looking perplexed. "It is almost incredible."

"Yes, and I am just as astonished by your report," his companion said, lifting the cover of the box and gazing upon the blazing stones. "They do look wonderfully real," she added, "and yet I can hardly believe, Mr. Cutler, that any one would be willing to purchase them and give me the value of diamonds."

"But the gentleman to whom I submitted them—a jeweler and an expert—made me an offer for them," and he named the sum.

"So much?" murmured the fair woman, flushing. "Ah, it would be such a help."

"This offer," Mr. Cutler resumed, "is to remain open to you for three days, and you can take them to him within that time if you see fit, and Mr. Arnold will give you the money."

Mrs. Bently made a sudden gesture of repulsion, her head drooped, a flush swept up to her brow, and tears rushed to her eyes.

"Poor little woman!" said Justin Cutler to himself, "it humiliates her to think of selling her jewels—of course it must."

Then he asked, after a moment of thought:

"Would you accept the amount that Mr. Arnold offered?"

"Why, yes, if—if you are sure that they are real, and think it would be right for me to do so," she answered, with a somewhat troubled expression on her fair face.

"Of course it will be perfectly right; the man knew what he was talking about, for, as I told you, he is a diamond expert, and he examined them with the utmost care."

"The amount would be very acceptable," said the fair widow, musingly, "and I shall be glad to sell them; but—"

"The thought of going personally to sell your jewels humiliates you," the generous-hearted young man added;

"then let me do it for you, and relieve you of the disagreeable task."

"How kind you are; how you read my very thoughts; but I do not like to trouble you," murmured the beautiful woman, with a quiver of her red lips and a thrilling glance. "And yet," she continued, "I must have money at once. I was going to my lawyer this morning to beg him to try and raise something for me in some way, for I must settle my bill here to-day. I have dismissed my maid and engaged a room at No. 10—street, and am going there this afternoon. Oh! Mr. Cutler, it is very hard to be obliged to confess my poverty," and she had to abruptly cease her remarks, in order to preserve her self-control, for she seemed upon the point of breaking down utterly.

"Mrs. Bently," said the young man, with sudden impulse, "let me relieve you from all unpleasantness; let me advance you the sum which Mr. Arnold named; then I can take the crescents to him and he will make it right with me."

A peculiar smile lingered about his lips as he concluded.

"That is exceedingly kind of you," Mrs. Bently said, gratefully, "but, truly, Mr. Cutler, I am almost afraid to take you at your word."

"Why?"

"Because I have always regarded the crescents as paste, and—and I cannot quite divest myself of the idea even now, in spite of your assurance," she answered, with a clouded brow.

Her companion laughed aloud.

"I will be responsible for their genuineness," he returned. "See!" he added, drawing a card from his pocket and writing rapidly upon it. "I will give you this to ease your conscience."

She took it and read:

"I, the undersigned, purchase of Mrs. Bently a pair of crescent ornaments which she affirms are paste, but which I am content to accept as genuine, for the sum agreed upon."

The price was carried out in figures, and his full name signed underneath.

She looked up at him with tears in her eyes.

"You are determined to befriend me, in spite of my scruples," she murmured, brokenly.

"I would gladly do a hundred-fold more for you," he replied, with tender earnestness. "Will you let me have the crescents now?"

"Yes, and thank you more than I can express," she answered, with drooping lids.

He drew forth a wallet filled with bills, and began to count out the sum he had named.

"Wait a moment," said Mrs. Bently, the color mounting to her temples; "I have a handsome case for the ornaments. I will go and get it for you."

She turned suddenly and vanished from his presence, before he could tell her he would rather take them in the little box.

"How sensitive the poor child is!" he murmured, with a tender smile; "she could not even bear to see me count out the money."

Mrs. Bently soon returned with a handsome morocco case in her hands.

"They look better in this," she remarked, as she lifted the lid, and revealed the crescents lying upon a rich black velvet bed; "and," with a nervous little laugh, "now that I know they are genuine, I really am very loath to part with them, in spite of my necessity."

She closed the case with a snap, and passed it to him, and he slipped a roll of crisp bank-bills into her hand.

"This arrangement will smooth all difficulties, I trust," he said, "and now," with a slight tremor in his voice, "I have a special favor to ask. May I come to see you at No. 10— street?"

"Certainly, you may, Mr. Cutler," she replied, lifting a bright, eager face to him, "and I assure you I shall have a warmer welcome for no one else. I cannot tell you how grateful I am—"

"Do not speak of that," he interposed. "I am amply repaid for anything I have done by seeing the look of trouble gone from your face. I must bid you good morning now, but I shall give myself the pleasure of calling upon you very soon."

He held out his hand to her, and she laid hers within it. He was surprised to find it icy cold and trembling, but he attributed it to emotion caused by the parting with him.

"Then I shall only say *au revoir*," she responded, smiling.

She looked so lovely that he longed to draw her within his arms and take a more tender leave of her, but again putting a curb upon himself, he simply bowed, and left her, when with a quick, elastic step, she swept up stairs to her own apartments.

Justin Cutler was very busy all the morning, and did not find time to go to the jeweler's until the afternoon.

He had no intention of disposing of the crescents—he simply wished to tell him that he had himself concluded to purchase them, and then ask the privilege of depositing them in Mr. Arnold's safe for a few days; for they were to be his gift to the woman he loved, if she received his suit with favor.

The gentleman was in, and his eyes lighted as his glance fell upon the case which Mr. Cutler laid upon the show-case, for he believed that, in purchasing the crescents, he was going to get an unusually good bargain.

"Ah," he remarked, "the lady has decided to dispose of the stones?"

"Yes; but—" Mr. Cutler began, when he suddenly stopped, and gazed, astonished, at the man.

He had taken the case, opened it, and started in dismay as he saw what were within, while a look of blank consternation overspread his face.

Then he turned sternly, almost fiercely, upon the young man.

"What is the meaning of this?" he demanded, in a threatening tone. "Did you imagine you could cheat me in this miserable way? You have got hold of the wrong customer if you did."

"What do you mean, sir?" inquired Mr. Cutler, amazed, but flushing angrily at being addressed so uncivilly.

"These are not the stones you brought to me yesterday," said Mr. Arnold, who was also very angry.

"Sir!" exclaimed Justin Cutler, aghast, but with haughty mien.

"They are nothing but paste," continued the jeweler, eyeing the beautiful crescents with disdain; "and," he added, menacingly, "I've a mind to have you arrested on the spot for attempting to obtain money under false pretenses."

Mr. Cutler grew pale at this with mingled anger and a sudden fear.

He reached across the counter and took the case from Mr. Arnold's hand.

He turned the stones to the light.

At the first glance they seemed to be all right—he could detect nothing wrong; for aught that he could see the crescents were the same which he had submitted to the merchant the day before. But as he studied them more closely the gleam of the gems was entirely different—the fire of the genuine diamond was lacking.

"Can it be possible that I have been duped, swindled?" he exclaimed, with white lips and a sinking heart.

"I should say, rather, that you were attempting to dupe and swindle some one else," sarcastically retorted the diamond dealer. "The stones are a remarkably fine imitation, I am free to confess, and would easily deceive a casual observer; but if you have ever tried and succeeded in this clever game before, you are certainly caught this time."

"Mr. Arnold, I assure you that I am blameless in this matter—that I honestly believed the jewels to be the same that I brought to you yesterday," the young man said, with an earnest directness which convinced the gentleman that he spoke the truth. "I see now," he continued, "that they are not; and"—a feeling of faintness almost overpowering him as he realized all that this experience would cost him, aside from his pecuniary loss—"I have been outrageously deceived and hoodwinked, for I have already advanced the sum you named to the woman who wished to dispose of the diamonds."

Mr. Arnold searched the manly face before him, and was forced to believe in the truth of his statements.

"If that is so, then you have indeed been wretchedly swindled," he said; "for these crescents are but duplicates in paste of those I examined yesterday. How did you happen to be so taken in?"

Mr. Cutler briefly related the circumstances, and when he concluded, Mr. Arnold remarked:

"The woman was an accomplished cheat, and led you on very adroitly. Your mistake was in advancing the money for the stones; if you had brought these things to me first, you would have saved yourself this loss. But of course she never would have allowed that; her game was to get the money from you, and she worked you finely for it."

Mr. Cutler groaned in spirit as he realized it all, and how he had tied his own hands by what he had written on the card that he had given to the wily woman.

Mrs. Georgie Sheldon

He kept this portion of the transaction to himself, however; he could not confess how foolishly weak he had been. Surely his infatuation for the beautiful widow had led him beyond all bounds of common sense and good judgment; but he had no one but himself to blame, and he must bear his loss as best he could. His lost faith in womanhood was the heaviest part of it.

"I sincerely regret having put you to so much trouble, Mr. Arnold," he courteously remarked, as he closed the jewel-case and put it out of sight, "and as a favor, I would ask that you regard this matter as strictly confidential. I have been miserably fooled, and met with a heavy loss, but I do not wish all Chicago to ring with the story."

"You may trust me, and accept my assurance that I am sincerely sorry for you," the jeweler returned, in a tone of sympathy, and now entirely convinced of the honesty of the young man. "And let me tell you," he added, "for your personal benefit, while examining those crescents yesterday, I put a private mark on the back of the settings with a steel-pointed instrument; it was like this"—making a cipher on a card and passing it to him. "If you should ever be fortunate enough to come across them again, you could identify them by it."

"Thank you," Mr. Cutler returned, as he put it carefully away.

Then he wished the gentleman a polite good-day, and went out of the store, a wiser, but a somewhat poorer, man than he had been the previous day.

He was almost crushed by the wrong which had been perpetrated against him. He had been thoroughly and artfully deceived. Mrs. Bently—if indeed that was her real name, which he doubted—had seemed such a modest and unassuming woman, so frank, and sweet, and ingenuous, that he would have indignantly resented it had any one hinted to him that she was not all that she appeared to be.

He had never met any woman who possessed such power to charm him, and yet she had never seemed to seek his notice—had never appeared to thrust herself upon him in any way. He had instead sought *her* and been especially attracted to her by the very simplicity and naturalness of her deportment; and this rude awakening to the fact of her duplicity was therefore far more bitter than the loss of his money, although that was considerable.

He was greatly depressed, but, on leaving Mr. Arnold's store, he proceeded directly to the street and number which she had given as her future place of residence. It proved to be an empty house with the sign "To Rent" staring at him from several windows.

He next sought for the lawyer who, Mrs. Bently had told him, had conducted her business affairs. There was no such person to be found.

Then, his indignation getting the better of his grief and disappointment, he sought a detective, told his story, and gave the case into his hands.

"Keep the matter quiet, Rider," he said, "but spare no expense to find the woman. If she is a professional thief, she will try the same trick on some one else; and though we may not be able to bring her to justice in this case, since I so rashly tied my hands by giving her that writing, yet I should like to give my evidence against her for the benefit of some other unfortunate victim."

Thus the matter rested for the time, and Justin Cutler once more threw himself heart and soul into business, vowing that he would never trust a woman again.

"But I'll keep the bogus crescents, to remind me of my folly, for of course I shall never see the real ones again."

Did he?

CHAPTER III

MONA

"Mona, come here, dear, please."

A gentleman, of perhaps forty-five, looked up from the desk where he had been writing, as he uttered this request; but his voice trembled slightly, and was replete with tenderness, as he spoke the name which heads this chapter.

The girl whom he addressed was sitting by a window on the opposite side of the room, and she lifted her bright brown head and turned a pair of dark, liquid eyes upon the speaker.

"Yes, Uncle Walter," she cheerfully responded, as, laying down her book, she arose and moved gracefully across the room toward the handsome, aristocratic-looking man at the desk, who watched her every motion with a fond intentness that betrayed a deep and absorbing affection for her.

He frowned slightly, however, as she spoke, and a half-bitter, half-scornful smile curled his finely chiseled lips for an instant.

The young girl was tall and exquisitely formed, but her face was one not easily described. Her features were delicate and

Mrs. Georgie Sheldon

clearly defined, yet with a certain roundness about them such as one sees in a faultlessly sculptured statue, while unusual strength of character was written indelibly upon them. Her hair was slightly curly, and arranged with a careful careless-ness that was very becoming, while here and there a stray ringlet, that had escaped the silver pin that confined it, seemed to coquet with the delicate fairness of her neck and brow.

Reaching her uncle's side, she laid one white hand upon his shoulder, then slid it softly about his neck.

"What is it, Uncle Walter? What, makes you look so sober? Have I done something naughty that you are going to scold me for?" she concluded, playfully, as she bent forward and looked archly into his eyes.

His face grew luminous instantly as he met her gaze, while he captured her small hand and toyed with the rosy, taper fingers.

"Do I look sober?" and a brilliant smile chased the gloom from lip and brow. "I did not mean to, while you know I could not scold you if you were ever so naughty, and you are never that."

"Perhaps every one does not look upon me with your partial eyes," the lovely girl returned, with a musical little laugh.

The man carried the hand he held to his lips and kissed it lingeringly.

"Let me see," he remarked, after thinking a moment, "isn't it somebody's birthday to-day?"

"So it is! but I had not thought of it before," exclaimed the maiden, with a lovely flush sweeping into her cheeks. "And," with a far-away look in her eyes, "I am eighteen years old."

"Eighteen!" and Walter Dinsmore started slightly, while a vivid red suddenly dyed his brow, and a look of pain settled about his mouth.

But he soon conquered his emotion, whatever it might have been, and strove to say, lightly:

"Well, then, somebody must have a gift. What would you like, Mona?"

She laughed out sweetly again at the question.

"You know I have very strange notions about gifts, Uncle Walter," she said. "I do not care much about having people buy me pretty or costly things as most girls do; I like something that has been made or worn or prized by the giver—something that thought and care have been exercised upon. The little bouquet of blue-fringed gentians which you walked five miles to gather for me last year was the most precious gift I had; I have it now, Uncle Walter."

"You quaint child!" said the man, with a quiver of strong feeling in his tone. "You would like something prized by the giver, would you?" he added, musingly. "Well, you shall be gratified."

He turned again to his desk as he spoke, unlocked and pulled out a drawer.

"Would you like this?" he asked, as he uncovered a box about eight inches square.

"Why, it is a mirror! and what a queer one!" exclaimed the

maiden, as she bent forward to look, and found her lovely, earnest face reflected from a square, slightly defaced mirror that was set in an ebony frame richly inlaid with gold and pearl.

"Yes, dear, and it once belonged to Marie Antoinette. Doubtless it reflected her face many times during the latter half of the last century, as it now reflects yours, my Mona," said Mr. Dinsmore.

"To Marie Antoinette?" repeated Mona, breathlessly, "to the Queen of France? and would you give it to me—*me*, Uncle Walter?"

"Yes, I have kept it for you many years, dear," the man answered, but turning away from her eager, delighted eyes and glowing face, as if something in them smote him with sudden pain.

"Oh! thank you, *thank* you! It is a priceless gift. What can I say? How can I show you how delighted I am?" Mona cried, eagerly.

"By simply accepting it and taking good care of it, and also by giving me your promise that you will never part with it while you live," Mr. Dinsmore gravely replied.

"Of *course* I would never part with it," the young girl returned, flushing. "The mere fact of your giving it to me would make it precious, not to mention that it is a royal mirror and once belonged to that beautiful but ill-fated queen. How did it happen to come into your possession, Uncle Walter?"

The man grew pale at this question, but after a moment he replied, though with visible effort:

"It was given to your great grandmother by a Madame Roquemaure, an intimate friend, who was at one time a lady in waiting at the court of Louis the Sixteenth."

"What was her name?" eagerly asked Mona—"my grandmother's, I mean."

"She was a French lady and her maiden name was Ternaux, and when her friend, Madame Roquemaure, died, she bequeathed to her this mirror, which once graced the dressing-room of Marie Antoinette in the Tuileries."

"What a prize!" breathed Mona, as she gazed reverently upon the royal relic. "May I take it, Uncle Walter?"

"Certainly," and the man lifted it from the box and laid it in her hands.

"How heavy it is!" she exclaimed, flushing and trembling with excitement, as she clasped the precious treasure.

"Yes, the frame is of ebony and quite a massive one," said Mr. Dinsmore.

"It looks like a shallow box with the mirror for a cover; but of course it isn't, as there is no way to get into it," observed the young girl, examining it closely.

Her companion made no reply, but regarded her earnestly, while his face was pale and his lips compressed with an expression of pain.

"And this has been handed down from generation to generation!" Mona went on, musingly. "Have you had it all these years, Uncle Walter—ever since you first took me?"

"Yes, and I have been keeping it for you until you should reach your eighteenth birthday. It is yours now, my Mona, but you must never part with it—it is to be an heir-loom. And if you should ever be married, if you should have children, you are to give it to your eldest daughter. And, oh! my child," the agitated man continued, as he arose and laid his hands upon her shoulders and looked wistfully into her beautiful face, "I hope, I *pray*, that *your* life may be a happy one."

"Why, Uncle Walter, how solemn you have grown all at once!" cried the young girl, looking up at him with a smile half startled, half gay, "One would think you were giving me some sacred charge that is to affect all my future life, instead of this lovely mirror that has such a charming and romantic history. I wish," she went on, thoughtfully, "you would tell me just how you came to have it. Did it descend to you from your father's or your mother's ancestors?"

The man sat down again before he replied, and turned his face slightly away from her gaze as he said:

"It really belonged to your mother, dear, instead of to me, for it has always been given to the eldest daughter on the mother's side; so, after your mother died, I treasured it to give to you when you should be old enough to appreciate it."

"I wish you would tell me more about my mother, Uncle Walter," the young girl said, wistfully, after a moment of silence. "You have never seemed willing to talk about her— you have always evaded and put me off when I asked you anything, until I have grown to feel as if there were some mystery connected with her. But surely I am old enough now, and have a right to know her history. Was she your only sister, and how did it happen that she died all alone in London? Where was my father? and why was she left so poor when you had so much? Really, Uncle Walter, I think I ought to insist upon being told all there is to know about my parents and myself. You have often said you would tell me some time; why not now?"

"Yes, yes, child, you are old enough, if that were all," the man returned, with livid lips, a shudder shaking his strong frame from head to foot.

Mona also grew very pale as she observed him, and a look of apprehension swept over her face at his ominous words.

"Was there anything wrong about mamma?" she began, tremulously.

"No, no!" Mr. Dinsmore interposed, almost passionately; "she was the purest and loveliest woman in the world, and her fate was the saddest in the world."

"And my father?" breathed the girl, trembling visibly.

"Was a wretch! a faithless brute!" was the low, stern reply.

"What became of him?"

"Do not ask me, child," the excited man returned, almost fiercely, but white to his lips, "he deserves only your hatred and contempt, as he has mine. Your mother, as you have been told, died in London, a much wronged and broken-hearted woman, where she had lived for nearly three months in almost destitute circumstances. The moment I learned of her sad condition I hastened to London to give her my care and protection; but she was gone—she had died three days before my arrival, and I found only a wee little baby awaiting my care and love."

A bitter sob burst from the man's lips at this point, but after struggling for a moment for self-control, he resumed:

"That baby was, of course, yourself, and I named you Mona for your mother, and Ruth for mine. The names do not go together very well, but I loved them both so well I wanted you to bear them, I gave you in charge of a competent nurse, with instructions that everything should be done for your comfort and welfare; then I sought to drown my grief in travel and constant change of scene. When I returned to London you were nearly two years old and a lovely, winning child, I brought you, with your nurse, to America, resolving that you should always have the tenderest love and care; and Mona, my darling, I have tried to make your life a happy one."

"And you have succeeded. Uncle Walter, I have never known a sorrow, you have been my best and dearest friend, and I love you—I love you with all my heart," the fair girl cried, as she threw her arm about his neck and pressed her quivering lips to his corrugated brow.

Mr. Dinsmore folded her close to his breast, and held her there in a silent embrace for a moment.

But Mona's mind was intent upon hearing the remainder of his story; and, gently disengaging herself, she continued:

"But tell me—there is much more that I want to know. What was the reason—why did my father—"

She was suddenly cut short in her inquiries by the opening of a door and the entrance of a servant.

"There is a caller for you in the drawing-room, Miss Mona,' the girl remarked, as she extended to her the silver salver, on which there lay a dainty bit of pasteboard.

Mona took it and read the name engraved upon it.

"It is Susie Leades," she said, a slight look of annoyance sweeping over her face, "and I suppose I must go; but you will tell me the rest some other time, Uncle Walter? I shall never be content until I know all there is to know about my father and mother."

"Yes—yes; some other time I will tell you more," Mr. Dinsmore said, but with a sigh of relief, as if he were glad of this interruption in the midst of a disagreeable subject.

"I will leave the mirror here until I come back," Mona said, as she laid it again in its box in the drawer; then, softly kissing her companion on the lips, she went slowly and reluctantly from the room.

The moment the door had closed after her, Walter Dinsmore, the proud millionaire and one of New York's most respected and prominent citizens, dropped his head upon the desk before him and groaned aloud:

"How can I ever tell her?" he cried. "Oh, Mona, Mona! I have tried to do right by your little girl—I have tried to make her life bright and happy; must I cloud it now by revealing the wrong and sorrow of yours? *Must* I tell her?"

A sob burst from him, and then for some time he lay perfectly still, as if absorbed in deep thought.

At length he lifted his head, and, with a resolute look on his fine face, drew some paper before him and began to write rapidly.

Mrs. Georgie Sheldon

At the expiration of half an hour he folded what he had written, put it in an envelope, and carefully sealed it, then turning it over, wrote 'For Mona" on the back.

This done he took up the mirror which he had but just given the young girl, pressed hard upon one of the pearl and gold points with which the frame was thickly studded, and the bottom dropped down like a tiny drawer, revealing within it a package composed of half a dozen letters and a small pasteboard box.

The man was deadly pale, and his hands trembled as he took these out and began to look over the letters.

But, as if the task were too great for him, he almost immediately replaced them in their envelopes, and restored them to the drawer in the mirror. Then he uncovered the little box, and two small rings were exposed to view—one a heavy gold band, the other set with a whole pearl of unusual size and purity.

"Poor Mona!" he almost sobbed, as he touched them with reverent fingers. "I shall never be reconciled to your sad fate, and I cannot bring myself to tell your child the whole truth, at least not now. I will tell her something—just enough to satisfy her, if she questions me again—the rest I have written, and I will hide the story with these things in the mirror; then in my will I will reveal its secret, so that Mona can find them. She will be older, and perhaps happily settled in life by the time I get through, and so better able to bear the truth."

He replaced the box and letters in the secret drawer of the mirror, also the envelope which contained what he had written, after which he carefully closed it, and returned the royal relic to the box in his desk.

"There! everything is as safe as if it were buried in Mona's grave—no one would ever think of looking for that history in such a place, and the secret will never be disclosed until I see fit to reveal it."

He had scarcely completed these arrangements when Mona re-entered the room, her face bright and smiling, a lovely flush on her cheeks, a brilliant light in her liquid brown eyes.

"Well, my pet, you look pretty enough to kiss," exclaimed Mr. Dinsmore, assuming a lightness of manner which he was far from feeling. "Have you had a pleasant call?"

"Indeed I have, Uncle Walter, and I have also had an invitation to attend the opera to-night," Mona replied, with increasing color.

"Ah! then I imagine that Miss Susie did not come alone, eh?" and Mr. Dinsmore smiled roguishly.

"No; Mr. Palmer was with her; and just as they were at the door, he discovered that he had forgotten his cards, so he just penciled his name on the back of Susie's; but I did not see it, and of course did not know he was here until I went into the drawing-room," the young girl explained.

"Palmer! Ray Palmer, the son of Amos Palmer, the diamond merchant?" questioned Mr. Dinsmore.

"Yes, I have met him a number of times during the past year, and at Susie's birthday party last week he asked permission to call. May I go to-night, Uncle Walter?" Mona asked, with downcast eyes.

"Who else is to be in the party?" gravely inquired her uncle.

Mrs. Georgie Sheldon

"Susie, and Louis, her brother."

"Then I have no objection to your going also," said Mr. Dinsmore; then he added, as he searched the beautiful face beside him: "I know that Ray Palmer is an exceptionally fine young man, and any girl might feel honored in receiving his attentions. Is he agreeable to you, Mona?"

A vivid scarlet suffused the maiden's face at this pointed question, and the gentleman laughed out softly as he beheld it.

"Never mind, dear," he continued, lightly. "I am already answered, and Mr. Ray Palmer has my best wishes for his future success and happiness. There, run back now, and tell your callers that you will join their party."

A shy, sweet smile wreathed Mona's lips as she again left the room.

But she was not gone, long—scarcely five minutes had elapsed before she returned, and gliding to Mr. Dinsmore's side, she said, with quiet resolution:

"Now, Uncle Walter, I want to hear the remainder of what you have to tell me about my father and mother."

CHAPTER IV

MONA ASKS SOME PERTINENT QUESTIONS

Mr. Dinsmore's face clouded instantly at Mona's request, but after thinking a moment, he threw back his head with a resolute air, and said:

"There is not so very much more to tell, Mona—it is the oft repeated story of too much love and trust on the part of a pure and lovely woman, and of selfish pleasure and lack of principle on the part of the man who won her. When your mother was eighteen—just your age to-day, dear—she fell in love with Richmond Montague, and secretly married him."

"Then she was *legally* his wife!" burst forth Mona, with pale and trembling lips. "Oh, I have so feared, from your reluctance to tell me my mother's history, that—that there was some shame connected with it."

"No—no, dear child; set your heart at rest upon that score. She was legally married to Richmond Montague; but his first sin against her was in not making the fact public. He was just starting on a tour abroad and persuaded her to go with him. He claimed that he could not openly marry her without forfeiting a large fortune from an aunt, whose only heir he was, and who was determined that he should marry the

Mrs. Georgie Sheldon

daughter of a life-long friend. She was in feeble health and wanted him to be married before he went abroad, as she feared she might not live until he should come back. This he refused to do, although he allowed her to believe that he intended to marry Miss Barton upon his return. But he did marry your mother, and they sailed for Europe.

"They spent a few months traveling together, but while they were in Paris, your father suddenly disappeared, and it became evident to your mother that she had been deserted. To make matters worse, the people of the house where they had been living became suspicious of her, accused her of having been living unlawfully, and drove her away. She was desperate, and went directly to London, intending to return to America, but was taken ill there, and was unable to go on.

"Three months later I learned, indirectly, of her wretched condition, and I hastened to her, as I have already told you, only to find that I was too late—she had died just three days before my arrival, and only a few hours after your birth. Oh, Mona! I was heartbroken, for she was all I had, and the knowledge of her wrongs and sufferings drove me nearly wild; but—I cannot live over those wretched days—I simply *endured* them then because I could not help myself. But, as time passed, I gradually learned to love *you*—you became my one object in life, and I vowed that I would do everything in my power to make your life happy, for your mother's sake, as well as for your own," he concluded in tremulous, husky tones, while tears stood in his eyes.

"Dear Uncle Walter, no one could have been more kind than you have been," the young girl said, nestling closer to him; "you have been both father and mother to me, and I am very grateful—"

"Hush, Mona! Never speak of gratitude to me," he said,

interrupting her, "for you have been a great comfort to me; you have, indeed, taken the place of the little girl who never lived to call me father—and—have helped me to bear other troubles also," he concluded, flushing hotly, while a heavy frown contracted, his brow.

Mona glanced at him curiously, and wondered what other troubles she had helped him to bear; but her mind was so full of her own family history she did not pay much attention to it then. The remark recurred to her later, however.

"There is one thing more, Uncle Walter," she said, after a thoughtful pause. "What became of my father?"

Her companion seemed to freeze and become rigid as marble at this question.

"I wish you would not question me any further, Mona," he said, in a constrained tone. "Your father forfeited all right to that title from you before your birth. Cannot you be satisfied with what I have already told you?"

"No, I cannot," she resolutely replied. "Where did he go? What happened to him after my mother died? Has he ever been heard of since?" were the quick, imperative queries which dropped from her lips.

"Oh, yes," said Mr. Dinsmore, replying to the last query; "he married Miss Barton—the girl his aunt had chosen for him—shortly after his return to this country. The woman had set her heart upon the match, and died a month after the marriage, leaving her nephew the whole of her fortune."

"Did he—my father—know that he had a child living?" demanded Mona, in a constrained tone.

"Certainly."

"And—and—" she began, with crimson cheeks and blazing eyes, then choked and stopped.

"I know what you would ask—'did he ever wish to claim you?'" supplemented her companion, a bitter smile curling his white lips. "I have never been asked to give you up, Mona," he continued, apparently putting it thus so as to wound her as little as possible; "but I should not have done so under any circumstances."

"Did he never offer to settle anything upon me out of his abundance?" the young girl asked, bitterly.

"No; no settlement, no allowance was ever made, I alone have cared for you. But do not grieve—it has been a very delightful care to me, dear," Mr. Dinsmore said, tenderly, while he stroked her soft hair fondly with a hand that was far from steady.

"Is the—man living now?" Mona demanded, a cold glitter in her usually gentle eyes.

Mr. Dinsmore threw out his hand with a gesture of agony at this question.

Then suddenly pulling himself together, he hoarsely responded:

"No."

But he turned his face away from her gaze as he said it.

"When and where did he die?"

"Do not ask me. Oh, Mona, for pity's sake, ask me nothing more. I cannot, I will not bear this inquisition any longer," the man cried, in a despairing tone.

The young girl's face blanched suddenly at this, and she turned a wild, startled look upon her companion, as a terrible suspicion flashed into her mind.

Had her uncle avenged her mother's wrongs?—was his hand stained with her father's blood, and was this the reason why he was so fearfully agitated in speaking of these things?

It was an awful thought, and for a moment, every nerve in her body tingled with pain. All her strength fled, and she dared not question him further on that point, for her own sake, as well as his.

There was a dead silence for several moments, while both struggled for the mastery of their emotions; then Mona said, in a low, awed tone:

"Just one thing more, Uncle Walter—is—his other wife living?"

"I believe so."

"Where is she?"

"I do not know."

"Did she care nothing for me?"

"No, she hated your mother, and you a hundred-fold on her account."

"That is enough—I have heard all that I wish," Mona said,

coldly, as she started to her feet and stood erect and rigid before him. "You said truly when you told me that the man deserved hatred and contempt. I do hate and scorn him with all the hate and strength of my nature. I am glad he is dead. Were he living, and should he ever seek me, I would spurn him as I would spurn a viper. But oh, Uncle Walter, you must let me lean upon you more than ever before, for my heart is very, very sore over the wrong that has been done my poor mother and me. How good you have been to me— and I love you—I will always love and trust you, and I will never ask you any more questions."

She flung her arms around his neck, buried her face in his bosom, and burst into a passion of tears. The sorrowful story to which she had listened, and the fearful suspicion which, at the last, had so appalled her, had completely unnerved her.

The man clasped her to him almost convulsively, though a strong shudder shook his frame, laid his own face caressingly against her soft brown hair, and let her weep until the fountain of her tears was exhausted, and he himself had become entirely composed once more.

"My dear child," he said, at last, "let these be the last tears you ever shed for the wrong done you. I beg you will not allow the memory of it to make you unhappy, my Mona; for as I have assumed a father's care for you in the past, so I shall continue to do in the future; you shall never want for anything that I can give you while I live, and all that I have will be yours when I am gone. I have made an appointment with my lawyer for the day after to-morrow," he went on, in a more business-like tone, "when I purpose making my will, giving you the bulk of my property. I ought to have done this before; but—such matters are not pleasant to think about, and I have kept putting it off. Now dry your tears, my dear; it pains me to see you weep. And here," he added, smiling, and forcing himself to speak more lightly, "I almost forgot that I had something else for your birthday. Come, try on these trinkets, for you must wear them to the opera to-night."

He took a case from his pocket as he spoke, and slipped it into her hands.

Mona looked up surprised.

"But you have already given me the mirror, Uncle Walter," she said. "I could not have anything that I should prize more."

"Ah, well, but I could not let a birthday go by without spending a little money on you," he returned, fondly; "so look at your gifts, and let me see how they will fit."

Mona obediently opened the case, and found within a pair of narrow gold bands, studded with diamonds, for her wrists.

"They are lovely," she cried, a smile of pleasure breaking over her face, "and—I really believe it is the very pair that I was admiring in Tiffany's window only a few days ago!"

"I shouldn't wonder—sometimes the fairies whisper maidens' wishes in older ears, eh?" Mr. Dinsmore archly returned, and glad to see the gloom fading from her face.

"The fairies are great tell-tales then, for you are continually anticipating my wishes," Mona replied. "But," she added, glancing at the clock, "I have some little things to attend to before going out this evening, and I must be about them. A thousand thanks for my diamonds," and she kissed him softly as she said it, "and I shall surely wear them to-night."

"And here is your mirror," he said, taking the box containing it from the drawer of his desk. "Remember your promise, dear, never to part with it."

"It shall never go out of my possession," she gravely replied, as she took it, and then quietly left the room.

She was very grave as she went slowly up stairs, and once or twice a long, sobbing sigh escaped her.

"Oh, why did such a thought ever come to me?" she murmured. "It is too dreadful, and I will not harbor it for a moment. He is good and noble—his whole life has been grand and above reproach, and I love him with all my heart."

That evening, about seven o'clock, Mona Montague went down to the elegant drawing-room of her uncle's residence, exquisitely clad for the opera.

Her dress was a fine black lace, of a delicate and beautiful pattern, made over old gold silk, with the corsage cut low and sleeveless, thus leaving her neck and arms to gleam like alabaster through the meshes of delicate lace. The heavy edging at the throat was just caught together with a shell of Etruscan gold, studded with diamonds. Costly solitaires gleamed in her ears, while her dainty wrists were encircled with Mr. Dinsmore's gift of the morning. Upon her head she wore a jaunty hat of black lace, surrounded by a wreath of old gold crushed roses, that contrasted beautifully with her clear, fair skin and dark eyes. Her face was bright with anticipation, her cheeks were slightly flushed, and she was a vision of loveliness to gladden the heart of any beauty-loving man.

"I have come down to receive your verdict, Uncle Walter," she remarked, smiling, and sweeping him a graceful courtesy, as he threw down his paper and arose to meet her,

"Will I do?"

His face lighted with love and pride as he ran his eye over her.

"Really, Mona," he said, "you make me almost wish that I were going to see 'Il Trovatore' with you in Ray Palmer's place. You are a very queen of beauty to-night."

Mona flushed as he uttered Ray Palmer's name, but she put up her lips to kiss him for his compliment, and at that moment the young man himself was announced.

His eyes lighted with admiration, as he approached to salute the beautiful girl, and a thrill of delight ran through him as he clasped the hand she so cordially extended.

He was several inches taller than Mona, and a young man of singularly noble bearing, and perhaps twenty-three years of age.

Dignity of character and sincerity of purpose were stamped upon every feature of his intelligent face, and gleamed from his frank, genial eyes, which met yours with a directness that won the heart and confidence at once, while his manner and bearing as well as every detail of his dress, betrayed the thorough gentleman.

Mr. Dinsmore smiled complacently as he marked the exchange of greetings between the two young people. He saw that Mona was deeply interested in her handsome escort, as her deepening color and drooping eyes plainly betrayed.

He followed them to the door, and wished them a genial good-night, after which he went back to his library, saying to himself:

"I could wish nothing better for her. If I can but see her safely settled in life, I should have little to fear for the future, in spite of the miserable past. Young Palmer is a fine fellow, and I will favor his suit with all my heart. Then, with my will signed and sealed, my mind will be at rest."

Alas! alas! "Man proposes and God disposes."

CHAPTER V

MONA'S APPALLING DISCOVERY

Mona Montague was very happy throughout that memorable evening as she sat beside Ray Palmer, and listened to the opera of "Il Trovatore."

The four young people occupied a proscenium box, and made a very interesting group. Many a glass was turned upon them, many an eye studied their bright, animated faces, and found the sight almost as entertaining as the scene being enacted upon the stage.

To Ray Palmer's partial eye the fair girl beside him was the most beautiful object in the world, for he loved her with all his heart, and he made up his mind to win her if it were possible.

When the opera was over, the quartet repaired to a fashionable *cafe*, where they had a delicious little supper, and spent another happy half-hour discussing the merits of "Il Trovatore"; then they separated to go to their homes.

"You have given me great pleasure this evening, Miss Montague," Ray Palmer remarked, as he lingered for a moment beside her at the door of Mr. Dinsmore's residence, and loath to bid her good-night.

"Then I am sure the pleasure has been mutual, Mr. Palmer, for I have enjoyed myself exceedingly," Mona replied, as she lifted her flushed and smiling face to him.

"You are very kind to give me that assurance," he returned, "and you embolden me to crave another favor. May I have your permission to call upon you occasionally?"

"I am only very happy to grant it; pray consider yourself welcome at any time," Mona answered, cordially, but dropping her eyes beneath his earnest look.

"Thank you; I shall gladly avail myself of your kindness," the young man gratefully responded; and then, with a lingering clasp of the hand, he bade her good-night and ran lightly down the steps.

With a rapidly beating heart and throbbing pulses, Mona softly let herself in with a latch-key, turned out the hall gas, which had been left burning dimly for her, and started to mount the stairs, when she espied a gleam of light shining beneath the library door.

"Why! Uncle Walter has not gone to bed yet! Can it be that he is sitting up for me?" she murmured. "I will go and tell him that I have come in, and get my good-night kiss."

She turned back and went quietly down the hall, and tapped lightly at the door. Receiving no response, she opened it, and passed into the room.

The gas was burning brightly, and Mr. Dinsmore was sitting before his desk, but reclining in his chair, his head thrown back against the soft, bright head-rest, the work of Mona's skillful fingers.

"He has fallen asleep," said the fair girl, as she went to his side and laid her hand gently upon his shoulder.

"Uncle Walter," she called, "why did you sit up for me? Wake up now and go to bed, or you will be having one of your dreadful headaches to-morrow."

But the man did not make or show any signs of having heard her.

He was breathing heavily, and Mona now noticed that his face was unnaturally flushed, and that the veins upon his temples were knotted and swollen.

A startled look swept over her face, and she grew white with a sudden fear.

"Uncle Walter!" she cried out, sharply, and trying to arouse him; "speak to me! Oh! there is something dreadful the matter with him; he is ill—he is unconscious!"

With a wild cry and sob of fear and anguish, she turned and sped with flying feet from the room.

A moment later she was knocking vigorously at the door of the serving-man's room, begging him to "get up at once and go for Doctor Hammond, for Mr. Dinsmore was very ill."

Having aroused James, she called the other servants, and then flew back to her idolized uncle.

There was no change in him; he sat and breathed just the same. Instinctively feeling that something ought to be done immediately for his relief, with trembling fingers she loosened his neck-tie, unbuttoned his collar, then drenching her handkerchief with water from an ice pitcher, she began to bathe his flushed and knotted forehead.

She imagined that this afforded him some relief, and that his breathing was not quite so labored, but his condition drove her nearly frantic with fear and anxiety.

James was very expeditious in his movements, and in less than half an hour returned with the family physician.

"Oh, Doctor Hammond, what is the matter with him?" Mona cried, with a sinking heart, as she saw the grave expression that settled over the doctor's face the moment he reached his patient's side.

"An apoplectic attack," he replied, thinking it best that she should know the truth, and so be somewhat prepared for what he feared must soon come.

The unconscious man was borne to his chamber, and everything which human skill could devise was done for him. He rallied somewhat toward morning, but Doctor Hammond gave them no hope that he would ever be any better, or even retain his consciousness for any length of time.

The whole of his right side was helpless, and his tongue was also paralyzed, so that he was entirely speechless.

His efforts to talk were agonizing to witness, for he appeared to realize that his hours were numbered, and seemed to have something special on his mind that he wished to make those around him understand.

Mona alone, who never left his side, seemed able to interpret something of his meaning, and she asked him question after question trying to learn his desire; but he could only slowly move his head to signify that she did not yet understand.

"Oh, what shall I do?" she moaned, in despair; then a bright thought flashed upon her. "Is there some one whom you wish to see, Uncle Walter?" she asked.

His eyes lighted, and a faint nod of the head told her that she had got hold of the right thread at last.

"Who is it?" she said, eagerly; then remembering his helplessness, she added: "I will say over the letters of the alphabet, and when I reach the right one you must press my hand."

This method proved more successful, and Mona finally spelled out the name of Graves.

"Graves—Graves," she repeated, with a puzzled look; then she cried, her face lighting: "Oh, it is Mr. Graves, your lawyer, whom you want."

Again the sufferer nodded, and weakly pushed her from him with his left hand to show that he wanted her to be quick about summoning the man.

In less than an hour Mr. Graves was in the sick-room, and by signs and questions and Mona's use of the alphabet, he finally comprehended that Mr. Dinsmore wished him to draw up a will for him, leaving everything he had to Mona.

While the lawyer was thus engaged in the library, the invalid tried to make Mona understand that there was something else he wished to tell her, and she spelled out the word "mirror."

Mrs. Georgie Sheldon

"Oh, you want me to remember my promise never to part with it—is that it, Uncle?" she asked.

"No," he signaled, and looked so distressed that the much-tried girl sobbed outright. But she quickly controlled her grief, and finally spelled the word "bring," though her heart almost failed her as she realized that his left hand was fast becoming helpless like the other so that she could scarcely distinguish any pressure when she named a letter.

But she flew to her room and brought the royal mirror to him, and he tried to make her understand that there was something he wished to explain in connection with it.

We who have learned the secret of it, know what he wanted, but he could not even lift his nerveless hand to show her the gilded point beneath which lay the spring that controlled the hidden drawer and its contents.

Mona asked him question after question, but all that she could elicit were sighs, while great tears welled up into the man's eyes and rolled over his cheeks; and when at last a groan of agony burst from him, she could bear it no longer, and went weeping from the room, bearing the ancient relic from his sight.

She remained in her own room a few moments to compose herself before going back to him, and during her absence, Mr. Graves went up to him with the will which he had hastily drafted.

Mr. Dinsmore had had some conversation with him, in a general way, about the matter previous to this, and so he had drawn up the instrument to cover every point that he could think of. He read it aloud, and Mr. Dinsmore signified his satisfaction with it, and yet he looked troubled, as if it did not quite cover all that he desired.

Doctor Hammond and the housekeeper were summoned to act as witnesses; then Mr. Graves placed the pen, filled with ink, within the sick man's fingers, for him to sign the will. But he could not hold it—there was no strength, no power in them.

In vain they clasped them around it, and urged him to "try;" but they instantly fell away, the pen dropped upon the snowy counterpane making a great, unsightly blotch of ink, and they knew that he was past putting his signature, or even his mark, to the will.

As he himself realized this, a shrill cry of despair burst from him, and the next instant he lapsed into unconsciousness from a second stroke.

"The end has come—he will not live an hour," gravely remarked Doctor Hammond, as his skilled fingers sought the dying man's feeble pulse.

In half that time Walter Dinsmore was dead, and Mona Montague was alone in the world.

We will pass over the next few days, with their mournful incidents and the despairing grief of the beautiful girl, who had been so sadly bereft, to the morning after the funeral ceremonies, when Mr. Graves, with Mr. Dinsmore's unsigned will in his pocket, called to consult with Mona regarding her uncle's affairs and her own plans for the future.

He found her in the library, looking sad and heavy-eyed from almost incessant weeping, her manner languid and drooping.

She was engaged in trying to make up some accounts which

the housekeeper had requested her to attend to, hoping thus to distract her mind somewhat from her grief.

She burst into tears as the lawyer kindly took her hand, for the sight of him brought back to her so vividly the harrowing scenes of that last day of her idolized uncle's life.

But she strove to control herself after a moment, and invited the gentleman to be seated, when he immediately broached the subject of his call.

"Perhaps you are aware, Miss Montague," he began, "that Mr. Dinsmore, on the morning of his death, tried to make his will, in which he stated his wish to leave you all his property; but he was unable to sign it; consequently the document cannot stand, according to law. I was somewhat surprised," Mr. Graves continued, looking thoughtful, "at his excessive anxiety and distress regarding the matter, as he had previously given me to understand that you were his only living relative. Still he might only have wished to make assurance doubly sure. Do you know of any heirs beside yourself?"

"No," Mona answered, "he had no relatives as near to him as I. There are, I believe, one or two distant cousins residing somewhere in the South."

"Then you are of course the sole heir, and will have the whole of his handsome fortune—the will would only have been a matter of form. Mr. Dinsmore was a very rich man, Miss Montague, and I congratulate you upon being the heiress to a large fortune," the lawyer continued, with hearty sincerity in his tone.

But Mona looked, up at him with streaming eyes.

"Oh! but I would rather have my uncle back than all the wealth of the world!" she cried, with quivering lips.

"True. I know that your loss is irreparable—one that no amount of money can make up to you," was the kind and sympathetic response. Then the man returned to business again, "But—do you mind telling me your age, Miss Montague?"

"I was eighteen the day before my uncle died," the stricken girl replied, with a keen heart-pang, as she recalled that eventful day.

"You are very young to have care of so much property," said the lawyer, gravely. "What would be your wish as to the management of it? You ought really to have a guardian for the next few years. If you will designate some one whom you would wish, and could trust to act as such, I will gladly assist in putting Mr. Dinsmore's affair in convenient shape for him."

"You are very good, Mr. Graves," Mona thoughtfully returned. Then she added, wistfully: "Why cannot *you* act as my guardian? I know of no one in whom I have so much confidence. Uncle Walter trusted you, and surely there can be no one who understands his affairs as well as you do."

The man's face lighted at this evidence of her trust in him.

"Thank you, Miss Mona," he said. "It is of course gratifying to me to know that you desire this, and I really think that Mr. Dinsmore would have suggested such an arrangement had he been able to do so; but of course I felt delicate about proposing it. Walter Dinsmore was a dear and valued friend, as well as my client, and, believe me, I feel a deep interest in you, for his sake, as well as your own. I will accept the trust, and do the best I can for you, my child, thanking you again heartily for your confidence in me."

He spent a long time, after that, talking over business matters and looking over some of Mr. Dinsmore's papers, and when at length he took his leave, Mona was really greatly comforted, and felt that she had found a true friend to rely upon in her loneliness.

CHAPTER VI

A BOLD AND CUNNING SCHEME

On the afternoon previous to Mr. Dinsmore's death a woman of perhaps sixty years alighted from an elegant private carriage before the door of a fine residence on West—street, in New York city.

She was simply but richly clad in heavy, lustrous black silk, and was a woman of fine appearance, although her face wore a look of deep sadness which seemed to indicate some hidden trouble or sorrow.

Her hair was almost white, but carefully arranged, and lay low upon her placid, but slightly wrinkled, brow in soft, silken waves that were very becoming to her. Her complexion was unusually clear and fair for one of her years, although it might have been enhanced somewhat by the fine vail of white tulle which she wore over it. She was tall and commanding in figure, a little inclined toward portliness, but every motion was replete with graceful dignity and high-bred repose.

After giving directions to her coachman to wait for her, she mounted the steps leading to the door, pausing for an instant to read the name, "R. Wesselhoff, M.D." engraved upon a

Mrs. Georgie Sheldon

silver plate, before ringing the bell.

A colored servant soon answered her call, and responded affirmatively to her inquiry if the noted physician was in, then ushered her into a small but elegantly appointed reception-room upon the right of the lofty hall.

Five minutes later an elderly and singularly prepossessing man entered and saluted his visitor in a gracious and respectful manner.

"Mrs. Walton, I suppose?" he remarked, just glancing at the card which she had given the servant.

The woman bowed, then observed, with a patient but pathetic sigh:

"I have called, Doctor Wesselhoff, upon a very sad errand, and one which I trust you will regard as strictly confidential."

"Certainly, madame; I so regard all communications made by my patients," the gentleman courteously responded.

"I have a son," madame resumed, "who has of late betrayed symptoms of the strangest mania, although he appears to be in perfect health in all other respects. He imagines that some gigantic robbery has been committed; sometimes he declares that bonds to a large amount have been stolen, at other times it is money, then again that costly jewels have disappeared; but the strangest phase of his malady consists in the fact that he accuses me, and sometimes other members of the family, of being the thief, and insists that he must have me arrested. This has gone on for some time, and I have been obliged to adopt every kind of device in order to keep him from carrying out his threats and thus creating a very uncomfortable scandal. This morning he became more violent than usual, and I felt obliged to take some decided step in regard to proper treatment for him; therefore my visit to you."

"It is a singular mania, truly," said the physician, who had been listening with the deepest interest to his companion's recital. "I think I never have met with anything exactly like it before in all my experience. How old is your son, Mrs. Walter?"

"Twenty-four years," the woman replied, with a heavy sigh; "and," she added, tremulously, "I cannot bear the thought of sending him to any common lunatic asylum. I learned recently that you sometimes receive private patients to test their cases before sending them to a public institution, and that you have frequently effected a cure in critical cases. Will you take my son and see what you think of his case—what you can do for him? I shall not mind the cost—I wish to spare nothing, and I do not wish any one, at least of our friends and acquaintances, to know that he is under treatment for insanity until you pronounce your verdict. He seems sane enough upon all other topics, except now and then he persists in calling himself by some other name, and I know he would be very sensitive, should he recover, to have his condition known. He does not even suspect that I am contemplating any such thing, and I shall be obliged to use strategy in bringing him to you."

Doctor Wesselhoff was evidently very deeply interested in the case; he had never heard of anything like it before, and all his professional enthusiasm was aroused.

He spent some time questioning his visitor, and finally decided that he would receive the young man immediately—to-morrow afternoon Mrs. Walton might bring him, he said, if she could conveniently arrange to do so.

"I think, perhaps, it will not be best for me to come with him myself," the lady said, after considering the matter for some time. "Truly," she added, with a sad smile, "I almost fear to go out with him, lest he put his threats into execution and have me arrested. But I think I can arrange with my sister, Mrs. Vanderbeck, to persuade him to come with her as if to call upon a friend."

The matter was arranged thus, and madame arose to take her leave, the physician accompanying her to the door and feeling deep sympathy for the cultured and attractive woman in her strange affliction.

The next day, about one o'clock—the day following Mona Montague's attendance at the opera with Ray Palmer, and only a few hours after Mr. Dinsmore's death, a brilliantly beautiful woman, who might have been forty-five years of age, entered the handsome store of Amos Palmer & Co., diamond merchants and jewelers.

She was exquisitely dressed in an expensive, tailor-made costume of gray ladies' cloth, with a gray felt bonnet trimmed with the same shade of velvet as her dress. Her hands were faultlessly gloved, her feet incased in costly imported boots, and everything about her apparel bespoke her a favorite of wealth and luxury.

Her appearance was the more marked from the fact that her hair was a deep, rich red, and curled about her fair forehead in lovely natural curls, while she wore over her face a spotted black lace veil, which, however, did not quite conceal some suspicious wrinkles and "crow's-feet," if that had been her object in wearing it.

She had driven to the store in a plain but elegant *coupe*, drawn by a pair of black horses in gold-mounted harness.

Her driver was apparently a man of about thirty years, and of eminently respectable appearance in his dark-green livery.

She approached a counter on entering the store, and, in a charmingly affable manner, asked to look at some diamonds.

As it happened, at that hour, one of the clerks was absent, and Mr. Amos Palmer was himself in attendance in his place, and politely served the lady, laying out before her a glittering array of the costly stones she desired to examine.

He saw at once that she was a judge of the gems, for she selected not the largest and most showy, but the purest and the best, and he could but admire her discernment and taste.

When she had made her selections, and she took plenty of time about it, chatting all the while with the gentleman in the most intelligent and fascinating manner, she remarked that she wished her husband to see them before she concluded her purchase.

"But," she added, thoughtfully, "he is something of an invalid, and not able to come to the store to examine them; have you not some one whom you could trust, Mr. Palmer, to take the stones to my home for his inspection? If he sanctions my choice he will at once write a check for their price, or the attendant could return them if they were not satisfactory."

"Certainly," Mr. Palmer graciously responded; "we frequently have such requests, and are only too willing to accommodate our customers. Will madame kindly give me her address?"

Madame smiled as she drew a costly card-case from her no less costly shopping-bag, and taking a heavy card with beveled edges from it, laid it upon the counter before the jeweler, remarking that she should like to have the clerk accompany her directly back in her own carriage, as she wanted the matter decided at once, for the diamonds were to be worn that evening if they suited.

"Mrs. William Vanderbeck, No. 98—street," Mr. Palmer read, and then slipped the card into his vest pocket, after which he beckoned a clerk to him.

"Ask my son to step this way a moment," he said.

The man bowed respectfully, bestowing an admiring glance upon the attractive woman on the other side of the counter, and then withdrew to a private office at the other end of the room.

A moment later Ray Palmer made his appearance and approached his father.

Mr. Palmer introduced his son to Mrs. Vanderbeck, mentioned her desire that some one be sent to her residence with the diamonds she had selected for her husband's approval, and asked if he would assume the responsibility.

The young man readily consented, for the duty was not an unusual one, and immediately returned to the office for his coat and hat, while his father carefully put up the costly stones in a convenient form for him to take, and chatted socially with the beautiful Mrs. Vanderbeck meantime.

When they were ready Ray slipped the package into one of the outside pockets of his overcoat, but retained his hold upon it, and then followed the lady from the store to her carriage, and the next moment they drove away.

The young man found his companion a most charming

woman. She was bright, witty, cultured and highly educated. She had evidently seen a great deal of the world, and was full of anecdotes, which she knew how to relate with such effect that he forgot for the time everything but the charm of her presence and conversation.

The drive was rather a long one, but Ray did not mind that, and was, on the whole, rather sorry when the carriage stopped, and Mrs. Vanderbeck remarked, in the midst of a witty anecdote:

"Here we are at last—ah—"

This last ejaculation was caused by discovering that she could not rise from her seat, her dress having been shut into the door of the *coupe*.

Ray bent forward with a polite "allow me," to assist her, but found that he could not disengage the dress.

Just then the coachman opened the door, but in spite of the young man's utmost care, the beautiful cloth was badly torn in the operation.

"What a pity!" he exclaimed, in a rueful tone.

But madame looked up with a silvery laugh.

"Never mind," she said lightly, "accidents will happen, and I ought to have been more careful when I entered the carriage."

Ray stepped out upon the sidewalk, where he stood waiting to assist his companion, who, however, was trying to pin the rent in her skirt together. Then gathering up some packages that were lying on the seat opposite, she laughingly inquired:

"Please may I trouble you with these for a moment?"

"Indeed you may. Pray excuse my negligence," Ray gallantly exclaimed, as he extended his hands for them.

She filled them both, and then gracefully descended to the ground.

"You can wait, James, to take Mr. Palmer back," she quietly remarked, as they turned to mount the steps of the residence before which they had stopped.

"Pray do not ask your man to do that, Mrs. Vanderbeck; I can take a car just as well," the young man exclaimed.

"No, indeed," she returned, with a brilliant smile, "I am sure it would be very uncourteous in me to allow you to do so after your kindness in coming with me."

She rang the bell, and the door was almost immediately opened by a colored servant, when the beautiful woman led the way to a small reception room on the right of the hall, where she invited her companion to be seated, while she went to arrange for the interview with her husband.

She glided gracefully from the room, and Ray, depositing upon the table the packages he held, began to remove his gloves, while he glanced about the elegant apartment, noticing its hangings and decorations and many beautiful pictures.

Presently a gentleman of very prepossessing appearance entered, and Ray, arising, was astonished to behold, instead of the invalid he had pictured to himself, a man in the prime of life and apparently in perfect health.

He bowed politely.

"Mr. Vanderbeck, I presume?" he remarked, inquiringly.

The gentleman smilingly returned his salute, without responding to the name, then courteously asked him to take a seat.

Ray took the proffered chair, and then observed, although he wondered why Mrs. Vanderbeck did not return:

"As I suppose you know, I have called, at the request of Mrs. Vanderbeck, to have you examine some—Good heavens!"

And he suddenly leaped from his chair as if shot from it by some powerful but concealed spring, his face as pale as his shirt bosom, great drops of cold perspiration breaking out upon his forehead.

He had put his hand in his pocket as he spoke, to take from it the package of diamonds, but—*it was gone*!

"Pray do not be so excited, my young friend," calmly observed his companion, "but sit down again and tell me your errand."

But Ray Palmer did not hear or heed him. He had rushed to the window, where, with a trembling hand, he swept aside the heavy draperies and looked out upon the street for the *coupe* in which he had been brought to that house.

It was not in sight, and the fearful truth burst upon him—he had been the victim of an accomplished sharper.

He had been robbed, and the clever thief had suddenly vanished, leaving no trace behind her.

CHAPTER VII

A DESPERATE SITUATION

For a moment all Raymond Palmer's strength fled, leaving him almost as helpless as a child, while he gazed wildly up and down the street, vainly searching for the woman who had so cunningly duped him, for he knew, if his suspicions were correct, the firm of Amos Palmer & Co. would lose thousands of dollars by that day's operations.

But the young man was no irresolute character. He knew that he must act, and promptly, if he would regain the treasure he had lost, and this thought soon restored strength and energy to both heart and limb.

"I have been robbed!" he cried hoarsely, as he rushed back to the table and seized his hat and gloves, intent only upon getting out upon the street to trace the clever woman who had so outwitted him. Doctor Wesselhoff was also a victim of the sharpers; for, of course, it will be readily understood that the whole matter was only a deeply laid and cunningly executed scheme to rob the wealthy jewelers of diamonds to a large amount. He was watching Ray's every movement with keenest interest, and with a resolute purpose written upon his intelligent face. He quietly approached him, laid his hand gently upon his arm, and his magnetic power was so strong that Ray was instantly calmed, to a certain extent, in spite of his exceeding dismay at the terrible and unexpected calamity that had overtaken him.

"My young friend," he said soothingly, "you say you have been robbed. Please explain yourself. There is no one in this house who would rob you."

Ray searched the man's face with eager, curious eyes. Then he shook off his hand with an impatient movement.

"Explain myself!" he repeated hotly. "I have had a small fortune stolen from me, and I believe that *you* are an accomplice in the transaction."

"No, no; I assure you I am not," returned the gentleman gravely, and exactly as he would have addressed a person whom he believed to be perfectly sane. "I was told that a caller wished to see me, and I find a man claiming that he has been robbed in my house. What do you mean? Tell me, and perhaps I can help you in your emergency."

The young man was impressed by his courteous manner, in spite of his suspicions, and striving to curb his excitement, he gave him a brief explanation of what had occurred.

His account tallied so exactly with the statements of his visitor of the previous day that Doctor Wesselhoff became more and more interested in the singular case, and was convinced that his patient was indeed afflicted with a peculiar monomania.

"Who was this woman?" he inquired, to gain time, while he should consider what course to pursue with his patient.

"I do not know—she was an utter stranger to me—never saw

her before. She called herself Mrs. Vanderbeck."

That was the name of the "sister" whom Mrs. Walton had told him she would send with her son, so the celebrated physician had no suspicion of foul play.

"And who are you?" he asked, searching the fine face before him with increasing interest.

"My name is Palmer," Ray answered. "I am the son of Amos Palmer, a jeweler of this city."

Doctor Wesselhoff glanced keenly at him, while he thought that, if he was mad, there was certainly method in his madness to make him deny his own name, and claim to be some one else.

The physician had always been a profound student, he was thoroughly in love with his profession, devoting all his time and energies to it, consequently he was not posted regarding the jewelers of New York, or, indeed, business firms of any kind, fore he did not know Amos Palmer—if indeed there was such a man—from any other dealer in the vanities of the world.

He firmly believed the young man before him to be a monomaniac of an unusual type, although he could plainly see that, naturally, he was a person of no ordinary character and intelligence.

"I regret very much that you should find yourself in such deep trouble," he remarked in his calm, dignified manner, "and if you have been decoyed here in the way you claim, you are certainly the victim of a very clever plot. Perhaps I can help you, however; just come this way with me. I will order my carriage, for of course you must act quickly, and we will try our best to relieve you in this unpleasant predicament."

"Thank you sir; you are very kind to be so interested," returned Ray, beginning to think the man had also been made a tool to further the schemes of the thieves, and wholly unsuspicious that he was being led still farther into the trap laid for his unwary feet. "My first act," he continued, "will be to go to the superintendent of police, and put the matter in his hands."

"Yes, yes—that would be the wisest course to pursue, no doubt. This way, Mr.—Palmer. It will save time if we go directly to the stable," and Doctor Wesselhoff opened a door opposite the one by which Ray had entered, and politely held it for him to pass through.

Ray, wholly unsuspicious, stepped eagerly forward and entered the room beyond, when the door was quickly closed after him, and the sound of a bolt shooting into its socket startled him to a knowledge of the fact that he was a prisoner.

A cry of indignation and dismay burst from him, as it again flashed upon him that his companion of a moment before must be in league with the woman who had decoyed him to that place.

He sprang back to the door, and sternly demanded to be instantly released.

There was no reply—there was not even a movement in the other apartment, and he was suddenly oppressed with the fear that he was in the power of an organized gang of robbers who might be meditating putting him out of the way, and no one would ever be the wiser regarding his fate.

He felt that he had been very heedless, for he did not even know the name of the street he was on. His fascinating companion had so concentrated his attention upon herself that he had paid no heed to locality.

He repeated his demand to be released, beating loudly upon the door to enforce it.

But no notice was taken of him, and a feeling almost of despair began to settle over him.

He glanced about the room he was in, to see if there was any other way of escape, when, to his dismay, he found that the apartment was padded from floor to ceiling, and thus no sound within it could be heard outside.

It was lighted only from above, where strong bars over the glass plainly indicated to him that the place was intended as a prison, although there were ventilators at the top and bottom, which served to keep the air pure.

The place was comfortably, even elegantly, furnished with a bed, a lounge, a table and several chairs. There were a number of fine pictures on the walls, handsome ornaments on the mantel, besides books, papers and magazines on the table.

But Ray could not stop to give more than a passing glance to all this. He was terribly wrought up at finding himself in such a strait, and paced the room from end to end, like a veritable maniac, while he tried to think of some way to escape.

But he began to realize, after a time, that giving way to such excitement would do no good—that it would be far wiser to sit quietly down and try to exercise his wits; but his mind was a perfect chaos, his head ached, his temples throbbed, his nerves tingled in every portion of his body, and to think calmly in such a state was beyond his power.

Suddenly, however, he became conscious of a strange sensation—he felt a peculiar influence creeping over him; it almost seemed as if there was another presence in the room—a power stronger than himself controlling him.

This impression grew upon him so rapidly that he began to look searchingly about the apartment, while his pulses throbbed less heavily, his mind grew more composed, his blood began to cool, and he ceased his excited passings up and down the floor.

All at once, in the wall opposite to him, he espied a hole about the size of a teacup, and through this aperture he caught the gleam of a pair of human eyes, which seemed to be looking him through and through.

Once meeting that gaze, he could not seem to turn away from it, and he began to feel very strangely—to experience a sense of weariness, amounting almost to exhaustion, then a feeling of drowsiness began to steal over him—all antagonism, indignation, and rebellion against the cruel fate that had so suddenly overtaken him appeared to be gradually fading from his mind, and he could only think of how tired he was.

"What can it mean?" he asked himself, and made a violent effort to break away from the unnatural influence.

He believed that those eyes belonged to the man whom he had met in the other room—that having hopelessly ensnared his victim he was now availing himself of a panel in the wall to watch and see how he would bear his imprisonment.

"Who and what are you, sir, and what is the meaning of this barbarous treatment?" he demanded; but somehow the tones of his own voice did not sound quite natural to him. "You are aiding and abetting a foul wrong," he went on, "even if you are not directly concerned in it, and I command you to release me at once."

There came no word of reply, however, to this demand; but those strange, magnetic eyes remained fixed upon him with the same intense, masterful expression.

He tried to meet them defiantly, to resist their influence with all the strength of his own will; but that feeling of excessive weariness only seemed to increase, and, heaving a long sigh, he involuntarily began to retreat step by step before those eyes until he reached the lounge, when he sank upon it, and his head dropped heavily upon the pillow.

The next moment his eyelids began to close, as if pressed down by invisible weights, though he was still vaguely conscious of the gaze of those wonderful orbs gleaming at him through the hole in the wall.

But even this faded out of his consciousness after another moment, and a profound slumber locked all his senses. Ray Palmer was hypnotized and a helpless prisoner in the hands of one of the most powerful mesmerists of the world.

CHAPTER VIII

THE HEIRESS BECOMES A SEAMSTRESS

Poor Mona Montague was almost heartbroken over the sudden death of her uncle. She could not be reconciled to her great loss, and grieved so bitterly and continuously that her health began to be affected, and she lost all her lovely color and became thin and weak.

With the exception of the housekeeper and servants, Mr. Dinsmore had been her sole companion for many years, and they had been all in all to each other, so that this loss was a terrible blow to her.

Mona had always been an especially bright child unusually mature for her years, and probably her natural precociousness had been increased by having had so much of the companionship of her uncle. He had always interested himself in all her pleasures and made a confidante of her in all things which he thought she could comprehend; so in this way she had become very thoughtful for others, while it had also served to establish a very tender comradeship between them.

He had gratified her every wish whenever he could consistently do so, and had taken care that she should have

Mrs. Georgie Sheldon

the best of advantages and the most competent teachers. His home, also, had been filled with everything entertaining and instructive, and thus to her it had been rendered the dearest and happiest place in the world.

But the charm and center of attraction were gone, now that he had been laid away, and, though she believed that his death had left her independently rich, the knowledge gave her no pleasure—in fact, she scarcely gave the subject a thought, except when it was forced upon her.

A fortnight had elapsed since Mr. Dinsmore died, and everything had moved on as usual in his elegant home, while Mrs. Marston, the housekeeper, strove in every way to comfort Mona and to keep her mind occupied so that her thoughts would not long dwell upon her bereavement.

But the young girl's condition troubled her greatly. She was listless and languid; she lost her appetite, and had seasons of depression and outbursts of sorrow that were really alarming.

Susie Leades came to her almost every day and tried to cheer her. Mona appreciated her kind efforts, and was somewhat comforted by them, while she also had many letters of sympathy and condolence from her numerous friends.

But to her great surprise Ray Palmer had never once come to inquire for her; neither had he written her one word to tell her that he felt for her in this bitter trial.

She was both grieved and hurt over his apparent indiffer-ence, especially after the request he had made on the evening of their attendance at the opera, and the many unmistakable signs of regard which he had betrayed for her at that time.

She was brooding over this one afternoon when Mr. Graves,

the lawyer and her future guardian, was announced.

He looked serious and troubled; indeed, he was so unlike himself that Mona observed it, and asked him if he was ill.

"No, Miss Mona, I am not really ill, but I am laboring under trouble and anxiety enough to almost make me so," he responded, as he took her extended hand and gazed down upon her own colorless face with a sorrowful, wistful look.

"Trouble?" she repeated, with a quivering lip. "Oh, trouble is so much harder to bear than illness."

"My poor child, your remark only makes my burden all the heavier," the gentleman returned, in an unsteady voice. "Alas, my trouble is all on your account, for I am the bearer of ill news for you."

"Ill news—to me?" exclaimed the young girl, in a wondering tone. "After losing Uncle Walter, it does not seem as if *any* trouble could move me; *nothing* can compare with that," she concluded, passionately.

"Very true; but there are other troubles in life besides death," said Mr. Graves, gently; "such as—the loss of fortune, poverty—"

"Do you mean that I am to have no fortune—that I am to be poor?" exclaimed Mona, astonished.

"Ah, I fear that it is so."

"How can that be possible? Uncle Walter was very rich, wasn't he? I certainly understood you to say so."

"Yes, I did; and I find, on looking into his affairs, that he was

Mrs. Georgie Sheldon

worth even more than I had previously supposed."

"Well, then, what can you mean? I am his only near relative, and you said that I should inherit everything," Mona said with a perplexed look.

"I know I did, and I thought so at that time; but, Mona, I was waited upon by a noted lawyer only a few days ago, and he claims the whole of your uncle's great wealth for another."

"Why, who can it possibly be?" cried the girl in amazement.

"Your uncle's wife, or, I should say, his widow."

"My uncle's wife?" repeated Mona, with a dazed look "Uncle Walter had no wife!"

"Are you sure?"

"Why, yes, of course. I have always lived with him, ever since I can remember, and there has been no one else in the family except the servants and the housekeeper. I am sure—I think—and yet—"

Mona abruptly paused as she remembered a remark which her uncle had made to her on her eighteenth birthday. He had said: "You have taken the place of the little girl who never lived to call me father, and—you have helped me to bear other troubles also."

Could it be possible, she now asked herself, that her uncle had had domestic troubles, that there had been a separation from his wife, and that this had been a life-long sorrow to him?

She had always supposed that his wife was dead, for he

would never speak of her, nor allow Mona to ask him any questions. From her earliest childhood she had somehow seemed to know that she must not refer in any way to such a subject.

"Ah, I see that you are in some doubt about it," Mr. Graves observed. "The matter stands thus, however: A woman, claiming to be Mrs. Walter Dinsmore, has presented her claim to her husband's property. She proves herself, beyond the possibility of doubt, to be what she pretends, bringing her marriage certificate and other papers to substantiate her title. She asserts that about a year after her marriage with Mr. Dinsmore they had trouble—of what nature I do not know— and the feeling between them was so irreconcilable they agreed to part, Mr. Dinsmore allowing her a separate maintenance. They were living in San Francisco at the time. There was no divorce, but they never met afterward, Mr. Dinsmore coming East, while she remained in California. She says there was a child—"

"Yes," Mona interposed. "Uncle Walter told me of the birth of a little girl, but that she never lived to call him father."

"I wonder what he meant by that?" said Mr. Graves with a start; "that the child came into the world lifeless? If such was the case, then your claim to the estate is still good."

"I supposed from what he said that it was born lifeless; still his words were somewhat ambiguous—even if she had lived several months, she might not have lived long enough to call him father!"

"Well, the woman asserts that the infant lived for a few hours, and brings the records to prove it, and claims that *she* is Mr. Dinsmore's only legitimate heir, through her child," Mr. Graves explained.

Mrs. Georgie Sheldon

"And is she?—is that true?" Mona asked.

"Yes, the court will recognize her claim—to all appearance, it is indisputable; and now I can understand what puzzled and troubled me when Mr. Dinsmore was so helplessly ill," Mr. Graves said, reflectively. "You doubtless remember how distressed he was when he tried to make me understand something in connection with his will."

"Yes," said Mona with streaming eyes. "Oh, poor Uncle Walter!"

"Doubtless he knew that his wife was still living," Mr. Graves resumed, "and that she would be likely to claim his property. He wanted *you* to have it—that I know—and he must have suffered untold anguish because he could not make me understand that he wanted to have me insert something in his will, which would provide against this woman's demands. Even if he had been able to sign the document which I drew up, she could have broken it, because she was not mentioned and remembered in it, and he knew this, of course."

"Then she will have all—I am not to have anything?" said Mona inquiringly, but without being able to realize, in the least, what such utter destitution meant.

"My poor child, she utterly refuses to release a dollar of your uncle's money to you. I have fought hard for you, Mona, for I could not bear to come to you with this wretched story; but she is inexorable. She seems, for some reason, to entertain a special spite—even hatred—against you, and asserts, through her counsel—*I* have not had the honor of meeting this peculiar specimen of womanhood—that you shall either work or beg for your bread; you shall have *nothing* of what legally belongs to her."

"Then I am absolutely penniless!" said Mona, musingly. "I wonder if I can make myself understand what that means! I have always had everything that I wanted. I never asked for anything that Uncle Walter did not give me if he could obtain it. I have had more money than I wanted to spend, and so I have given a great deal away. It will seem *very* strange to have an empty purse. I wonder where I shall get my clothes, when what I have are worn out. I wonder how I am to get what I shall need to *eat*—does it cost very much to feed one person? Why, Mr. Graves!" putting her hand to her head in a half-dazed way. "I *cannot* make it seem *real*—it is like some dreadful dream!"

"Mona, my dear child, do not talk like that," said the man, looking deeply distressed, "for, somehow, I feel guilty, as if I were, in a measure, responsible for this fresh calamity that has befallen you; and yet I could not help it. If I had only *known* that Mr. Dinsmore's wife was living, I could have made the will all right. Ah! no, no! what am I saying? Even if I *had*, he could not have signed it, for his strength failed. Still, I know that he wanted you to have all, and it is not right that this woman should get it from you."

"Must I go away from my home and from all these lovely things of which Uncle Walter was so fond?" Mona asked, looking about the beautiful room with inexpressible longing written on her young face. "Will she claim his books and pictures, and even this dear chair, in which I loved to see him sit, and which seems almost like a part of himself, now that he is gone?" and unable to bear the thought of parting from these familiar objects, around which clustered such precious associations, the stricken girl bowed her face upon the arm of Mr. Dinsmore's chair, and burst into a passion of tears.

"My dear girl, don't!" pleaded the tender-hearted lawyer, as he gently stroked her rich, brown hair with one hand, and wiped the tears from his own eyes with the other, "it almost breaks my heart to think of it, and I promise that you shall at least have some of the treasures which you prize so much. You shall not want for a home, either—you shall come to me. Mr. Dinsmore was my dear and valued friend, and for his sake, as well as your own, you shall never want for enough to supply your needs. I have not great wealth, but what I have I will share with you."

Mona now lifted her head, and wiped her tears, while she struggled bravely to regain her self-possession.

"You are very kind, Mr. Graves," she said, when she could speak, and with a newly acquired dignity, at which her companion marveled, "and I am very grateful to you for your sympathy and generosity; but I could never become an object of charity to any one. If it is so ordered, that I am to be bereft of the home and fortune which Uncle Walter wished me to have, I must submit to it, and there will doubtless be some way provided to enable me to live independently. It is all so new and so—so almost incomprehensible, that, for the moment, I was overcome. I will try not to be so weak and childish again; and now," pausing for a deep breath, "will you please explain to me just my position? When must I go, and—and can I take away the things that Uncle Walter has given to me from time to time? The pictures in my own rooms were given to me on certain birthdays and holidays; the piano he gave me new last Christmas, and I have a watch and some valuable jewelry."

"Of course, you may keep all such things," Mr. Graves answered with emotion, for it was inexpressively sad to have this girl so shorn of all that had made life beautiful to her so many years, "unless," he added, "it be the piano, and that you may have if there is any way to prove that it was given to you. You are to have a week in which to make your arrangements, and at the end of that time everything will pass into the possession of madame."

"Only a week longer in my dear home!" broke from the quivering lips of the stricken girl; "how can I bear it? Oh, Uncle Walter! how can I bear to have strangers handle with careless touch the things that you and I have loved so much? these dear books that we have read together—the pictures that we selected and never tired of studying to find new points for each other! Oh, every one is sacred to me!"

The strong man at her side was so moved by her grief that he was obliged to rise and walk to a window to conceal his own emotion.

But after a little she controlled herself again, and discussed everything with him in a grave, quiet, yet comprehensive way that made him sure she would in time rise above her troubles and perhaps become all the stronger in character for having been thus tried in the furnace of affliction.

He went every day after that to assist her in her arrangements for leaving; helped her to pack the treasures she was to take away with her, and to put in the nicest order everything she was to leave; for on this point she was very particular. She had secretly resolved that her uncle's discarded wife should have no fault to find with his home.

When the end of the week arrived Mr. Graves tried to persuade Mona to go home with him and remain until she could decide what she wished to do in the future, or, he told her, she was welcome to remain and make it her home indefinitely.

But she quietly thanked and informed him that she had already arranged to go as seamstress to a lady on West Forty-

Mrs. Georgie Sheldon

ninth street.

"You go as a seamstress?" exclaimed the lawyer, aghast. "What do you know about sewing—you who have always had everything of the kind done for you?"

"Oh, no; not everything," said Mona, smiling slightly. "I have always loved to sew since I was a little child, and my nurse made me do patchwork; and I assure you that I am quite an expert with my needle in many ways."

"But to go out and make it a business! I cannot bear the thought! What would your uncle say?" objected good Mr. Graves.

"I do not believe that Uncle Walter would wish me to be dependent upon any one, if it was possible for me to take care of myself," Mona gravely replied. "At all events," she continued, with a proud uplifting of her pretty brown head, "I could never allow another to provide for my needs without first trying my best to earn my own living—though, believe me, I am very grateful for your kindness."

"You are a brave and noble girl, Mona, and I admire your spirit; but—I have no daughter of my own, and, truly, both my wife and I would be glad to have you come to us," Mr. Graves urged, regarding her anxiously.

"Thank you; it is very comforting to know that you are so kindly disposed toward me, but I know that I shall respect myself more if I try to do something for my own support," was the firm yet gentle response.

Mr. Graves sighed, for he well knew that this delicately reared girl had a hard lot before her if she expected to earn her living as a sewing girl.

"At least you will regard me as your stanch friend," he said, "and promise me, Mona, that if you ever get into any difficulty you will appeal to me; that if you should find that you have undertaken more than your strength will allow you to carry out you will make my home your refuge."

"Yes, I will," she said, tears of gratitude starting to her lovely eyes, "and I am greatly comforted to know that I have one such true friend in my trouble."

"What is the name of the family into which you are going?" her companion inquired.

"I do not know, and it is a little singular that I do not," Mona replied, smiling. "I applied at an employment bureau for a situation a few days ago; yesterday I went to ascertain if there was a place for me and was told that a lady living on West Forty-ninth street wanted a seamstress, and I am to meet her at the office this afternoon. I, of course, asked the name, but the clerk could not tell me—she had lost the lady's card, and could only remember the street and number."

"Rather a careless way of doing business," the lawyer remarked, as he arose to go. "However," he added, "let me know how you succeed after you get settled, and if anything should occur to throw you out of your place, come straight to us, and make our home headquarters while you are looking out for another."

Mona's self-possession almost forsook her as she took leave of him. It seemed almost like losing her only friend, to let him go; but she bade him good-by with as brave a front as possible, though she broke down utterly the moment the door closed after him.

The remainder of the day was spent in packing her trunk and

Mrs. Georgie Sheldon

looking her last upon the familiar objects of the home that had always been so dear to her.

But her severest trial came when she had to bid the housekeeper and the servants farewell, for the loved and loving girl had been a great favorite with them all, and their grief was as deep and sincere at parting with her.

This over, she stepped across the threshold of Walter Dinsmore's elegant home for the last time, and entered the carriage that was to bear her away, her heart nearly bursting with grief, and tears streaming in torrents over her cheeks.

CHAPTER IX

MONA RECEIVES A SHOCK

When Mona arrived at the office of the employment bureau, at the hour appointed, she found awaiting her the carriage belonging to the woman who had engaged her services.

A pretty serving girl admitted her when she arrived at the elegant brown stone mansion, and remarked, as she showed her up to the room she was to occupy, that "the mistress had been called out of town for the day, and would not be at home until dinner time."

The girl seemed kindly disposed, and chatted socially about the family, which consisted only of "the mistress and her nephew, Master Louis." The mistress was a widow, but very gay—very much of a society lady, and "handsome as a picture," She was upward of forty, but didn't look a day over thirty. She was very proud and high spirited, but treated her help kindly if they didn't cross her.

Somehow Mona did not get a very favorable impression of her employer from this gossipy information; but her fate was fixed for the present, and she resolved to do the best that she could, and not worry regarding the result.

　　　　　Mrs. Georgie Sheldon

As the girl was about to leave the room to go about her duties, she remarked that dinner would be served at six o'clock, and that Mona was to come down to the basement to eat with the other servants.

Mona flushed hotly at this information. Must she, who all her life had been the petted child of fortune, go among menials to eat with she knew not whom?

But she soon conquered her momentary indignation, for she realized that she was nothing more than a servant herself now, and could not expect to be treated as an equal by her fashionable employer.

"Will you tell me your name, please?" she asked of the girl, and trying not to betray any of her sensitiveness.

"Mary, miss," was the respectful reply, for the girl recognized that the new seamstress was a lady, in spite of the fact that she was obliged to work for her living.

"Thank you; and—will you please tell me the name of your mistress, also; the card which she left at the office was lost, and I have not learned it," Mona said as she arose to hang her wraps in the closet.

"Lor', miss! that is queer," said the girl in a tone of surprise, "that you should engage yourself and not know who to."

"It didn't really make much difference what the name was— it was the situation that I wanted," Mona remarked, smiling.

"True enough, but my lady's name's a high-sounding one, and she's not at all backward about airing it; it rolls off her sweet tongue as easy as water off a duck's back—Mrs. Richmond Montague," and the girl tossed her head and drew herself up in imitation of her mistress's haughty air in a way that would have done credit to a professional actress, "But there," she cried, with a start, as a shrill voice sounded from below, "cook is calling me, and I must run."

She tripped away, humming a gay tune, while Mona sank, white and trembling, upon the nearest chair.

"Mrs. Richmond Montague!" she repeated, in a scarcely audible voice. "Can it be possible that she—this woman, to whom I have come as a seamstress—is my father's second wife—or was, since she is a widow! How strange! how very strange that I, of all persons, should have been fated to come here! It is very unfortunate that I could not have known her name, for, of course, I should never have come if I had. It may be," she went on, musingly, "that she is some other Mrs. Montague; but no—it could hardly be possible that there are two persons with that peculiar combination of names. This, then, is the woman for whom my father deserted my mother in order to secure the fortune left by his aunt! How unworthy!—how contemptible! I am glad that I fell to Uncle Walter's care; I am glad that I never knew him—this unnatural father who never betrayed the slightest interest in his own child. But—can I stay here with her?" she asked, with burning cheeks and flashing eyes. "Can I—his daughter—remain to serve the woman who usurped my mother's place, who is living in affluence upon money which rightly belongs to me?"

The young girl was trembling with nervous excitement, and a feeling of hot anger, a sense of deep injustice burned within her.

This startling discovery—for she was convinced that there could be but one Mrs. Richmond Montague—stirred her soul to its lowest depths. She felt a strange dread of this woman; a feeling almost of horror and aversion made her sink from contact with her; and yet, at the same time, she experienced an unaccountable curiosity to see and know something of her. There was a spice of romance about the situation which prompted her, in spite of her first impulse to flee from the house—to stay and study this gay woman of the world, who was so strangely connected with her own life.

She could leave at any time, she told herself, should the position prove to be an uncongenial one; but since she had chosen the vocation of a seamstress, she might as well sew for Mrs. Richmond Montague as any one else; while possibly she might be able to learn something more regarding her mother's history than she already knew. She felt sure that her uncle had kept something back from her, and she so longed to have the mystery fully explained.

But, of course, if she remained, it would never do for her to give her own name, for this woman would suspect her identity at once, and probably drive her out into the world again. It was not probable that she would knowingly tolerate the child of a rival in her home.

Mona was glad now that she had not told Mary her name, as she had once been on the point of doing.

"What shall I call myself?" she mused. "I do not dare to use Uncle Walter's name, for that would betray me as readily as my own; even Mona, being such an uncommon name, would also make her suspect me. There is my middle name, Ruth, and my father was called Richmond—suppose I call myself Ruth Richards?"

This rather pleased her, and she decided to use it. But she was strangely nervous about meeting Mrs. Montague, and several times she was tempted to send Mary for a carriage and flee to Mr. Graves's hospitable home, and start out from there to seek some other position.

Once she did rise to call her. "I cannot stay," she said. "I must go." But just then she heard voices in the hall below, and, believing that Mrs. Montague had returned, she turned back and sat down again with a sinking heart, assured that her resolve had come too late.

At six o'clock she went down to the basement, where she had been told dinner would be served, and where she found no one save Mary and Sarah, the cook, who proved to be a good-natured woman of about thirty-five years, and who at once manifested a motherly interest in the pretty and youthful seamstress.

Mary informed her, during the meal, that Mrs. Montague was going out that evening to a grand reception, and had sent word that she could not see her until the next morning; but that she would find some sheets and pillow slips in the sewing room, which she could begin to work upon after breakfast, and she would lay out other work for her later.

Mona uttered a sigh of relief over the knowledge that the meeting, which she so much dreaded, was to be postponed a little, and after dinner she returned to her room, and sat down quite composedly to read the morning paper, which she had purchased on her way to Mrs. Montague's.

While thus engaged, her eye fell upon the following paragraph:

"No clew has as yet been obtained to the mysterious Palmer affair, although both the police and detectives are doing their utmost to trace the clever thief. It is most earnestly hoped that they will succeed in their efforts, as such successful

Mrs. Georgie Sheldon

knavery is an incentive to even greater crimes."

"What can it mean?" Mona said to herself; "and what a blind paragraph! Of course, it refers to something that has been previously published, and which might explain it. Can it be that Mr. Palmer's jewelry store has been robbed?"

This, of course, led her thoughts to Ray Palmer, and she fell into troubled musings regarding his apparent neglect of her, and in the midst of this there came a rap upon her door.

She arose to open it, and found Mary standing outside.

"Please, Miss Richards, will you come down to Mrs. Montague's room?" she asked. "She has ripped the lace flounce from her reception dress while putting it on, and wants you to repair it for her."

Mona was somewhat excited by this summons; but, unlocking her trunk, she found her thimble, needles, and scissors, and followed Mary down stairs to the second floor and into a large room over the drawing-room.

It was a beautiful room, most luxuriously and tastefully fitted up as a lady's boudoir, and was all ablaze with light from a dozen gas jets.

In the center of the floor there stood a magnificently beautiful woman.

She was a blonde of the purest type, and Mona thought that Mary had made a true statement when she had said that, though she was upward of forty, she did not look a day over thirty, for she certainly was a very youthful person in appearance.

Her skin was almost as fair as marble, with a flush on her round, velvet-like cheeks that came and went as in the face of a young girl. Her features were of Grecian type, her hair was a pale gold and arranged in a way to give her a regal air; her eyes were a beautiful blue, her lips a vivid scarlet, while her form was tall and slender, with perfect ease and grace in every movement.

"How lovely she is!" thought Mona. "It does not seem possible that she could have even an unkind thought in her heart. I can hardly believe that she ever knew anything of my poor mother's wrongs."

Mrs. Montague was exquisitely dressed in a heavy silk of a delicate peach ground, brocaded richly with flowers of a deeper shade. This was draped over a plain peach-colored satin petticoat, and trimmed with a deep flounce of finest point lace. The corsage was cut low, thus revealing her beautiful neck, around which there was clasped a necklace of blazing diamonds.

Her arms were bare to the shoulder, the dress having no sleeves save a strap about two inches wide, into which a frill of costly point was gathered. Long gloves of a delicate peach tint came above her elbow, and between the top of each of these and the frill of lace there was a diamond armlet to match the necklace.

Magnificent solitaires gleamed in her ears, and there was a star composed of the same precious stones among the massive braids of her golden hair.

She was certainly a radiant vision, and Mona's quick glance took in every detail of her dress while she was crossing the room to her side.

Mrs. Georgie Sheldon

Mrs. Montague bent a keen look upon her as she approached, and she gave a slight start as her eyes swept the delicately chiseled face of the girl.

"You are the new seamstress, Mary tells me. What is your name—what shall I call you?" she questioned, abruptly.

"M—" Mona had almost betrayed herself before she remembered the need of concealing her identity.

But quickly checking herself, she cried:

"Ruth Richards, madame; call me Ruth, if you please."

"Hum! Ruth Richards—that's rather pretty," remarked the lady, but still searching the fair face before her with a look of curious interest. "But," she added, "you look very young; I am afraid you are hardly experienced enough to be a very efficient seamstress," and the lady told herself that those delicate, rose-tipped fingers did not look as if they had been long accustomed to the use of a needle.

"I do not understand very much about dressmaking," Mona frankly replied, although she ignored the reference to her youthfulness; "but I can do plain sewing very nicely, and, indeed, almost anything that is planned for me. I distinctly stated at the office that I could neither cut nor fit."

"Well, I can but give you a trial," with a little sigh of disappointment, as if she regretted having engaged one so young; "and if you cannot fill the place, I shall have to try again, I suppose. But, see here! I caught the thread that fastened this lace to my skirt, and have ripped off nearly half a yard. I want you to replace it for me, and you must do it quickly, for I am a little late, as it is."

Mona dropped upon her knees beside the beautiful woman, threaded her needle with the silk which Mary brought her, and, though her fingers trembled and her heart beat with rapid, nervous throbs, she quickly repaired the damage, and in a manner to win commendation from Mrs. Montague.

"You are very quick with your needle, and you have done it very nicely," she said, with a smile that revealed two rows of the most perfect teeth that Mona had ever seen. "And now tell me," she added, as she turned slowly around, "if everything about my costume is all right, then you may go."

"Yes," Mona returned; "it is perfect; it fits and hangs beautifully."

"That is the highest praise any one could give," Mrs. Montague responded, with another brilliant smile; "and I believe you are really a competent judge, since your own dress hasn't a wrinkle in it. Did you make it yourself?"

"I—I helped to make it. I told you I do not know how to fit," Mona answered, with a quick flush, and almost a feeling of guilt, for she had really done but very little work upon the simple black robe which had been made since her uncle's death.

"Well, I shall soon find out how much you do know," said the lady in a business-like tone. "You can begin upon those sheets and pillow slips to-morrow morning—Mary has told you, I suppose. That will be plain sewing, and you can manage it well enough by yourself. Now you may go," and the elegant woman turned to her dressing-case, gathered up an exquisite point-lace fan and handkerchief, while Mona stole softly out of the room and up to her own, where, no longer able to control the nervous excitement under which she was laboring, she wept herself to sleep.

The poor grief-stricken girl felt very desolate on this, her first night beneath a strange roof, and realized, as she had not before, that she was utterly alone in the world, and dependent upon the labor of her own hands for her future support.

Aside from the grief which she experienced in losing her uncle and the lovely home which for so many years had been hers, she was both wounded and mortified because of Ray Palmer's apparent indifference.

She could not understand it, for he had always seemed so innately good and noble that it was but natural she should expect some evidence of sympathy from him.

He had been so marked in his attentions to her during that evening at the opera, he had appeared so eager for her permission to call, and had implied, by both words and manner, that he found his greatest pleasure in her society, she felt she had a right to expect some condolence from him.

She had begun to believe—to hope that he entertained a more tender sentiment than that of mere friendship for her, and she had become conscious that love for him—and the strongest passion of her nature—had taken deep root in her own heart.

How kind he had been to her that night—how thoughtful! anticipating her every wish! How his glance and even the tones of his voice had softened and grown tender whenever their eyes had met, or he had spoken to her!

What, then, could be the meaning of his recent neglect? Could it be possible that it had been occasioned by the loss of her wealth?—that it had been simply the heiress of the wealthy Mr. Dinsmore in whom he had been interested, and now, having lost all, his regard for her had ceased?

It was a bitter thought, but she could assign no other reason for his strange silence and absence during her sorrow.

Must she resign all the sweet hopes that had begun to take form in her heart?—all the bright anticipations in which he had borne so conspicuous a part?

Must she lose faith in one who had appeared to be so manly, so noble, and so high-minded?

It certainly seemed so, and thus the future looked all the darker before her, for, humiliating as it was to confess it, she knew that Ray Palmer was all the world to her; that life without him would be almost like a body without a soul, a world without a sun.

Her uncle's death had come upon her so like a thunderbolt out of a clear sky, almost benumbing all her faculties with the grief it had hurled upon her so remorselessly, that she could think of nothing else until Mr. Graves had come to her with that other fatal piece of news—the loss of her fortune.

She had scarcely looked into a daily paper until that evening, for she felt no interest in the outside world; she could apply her mind to nothing but her own afflictions; consequently, she had not known anything of the mysterious and exciting circumstances connected with Ray Palmer's sudden disapp-earance and the stolen diamonds. That little blind paragraph, which she had seen just before she was called down to Mrs. Montague's room, was the only hint that she had had of any trouble or loss in the Palmer family.

So, of course, it is not strange that she so misjudged Ray; she could not know that only a great wrong kept him from

Mrs. Georgie Sheldon

speeding to her side to express the deepest interest and sympathy for her in her sorrow.

And it was well, perhaps, that she did not know, for it would only have added to her troubles and caused her greater suffering.

CHAPTER X

MONA MEETS MRS. MONTAGUE'S NEPHEW

The next morning, as soon as she had finished her breakfast, Mona asked Mary to conduct her to the sewing-room, and there she found a pile of work, which would have been exceedingly disheartening to a less resolute spirit.

But the young girl had bravely determined to do the best she could and not worry about the result.

Fate had willed that she must work for her living, and she had resolved not to murmur at her lot, but, putting forth all her energies, hope to please her employer and meet with success in her undertaking.

So she arranged her chair and table by a pleasant window overlooking the street, and then boldly attacked the mountain before her.

"I wonder if Mrs. Montague intends to have these done by hand or machine?" she mused, as she shook out the folds of snowy cloth and began to turn a hem on one of the sheets. "And then"—with a puzzled expression—"how am I to know how broad to make the hems?"

Mrs. Georgie Sheldon

She feared to go on with the work without special directions, for she might make some mistake. But after considering the matter, she determined to leave the sheets altogether and do the over-and-over sewing on the pillow-slips, until she could ascertain Mrs. Montague's wishes.

Mona was naturally quick in all her movements, and, being also very persevering, she had accomplished considerable by ten o'clock, when Mrs. Montague, in an elegant morning *negligee* of light-blue cashmere, and looking as lovely as an houri, strolled languidly into the sewing-room to see what her new seamstress was about.

"Oh, you are sewing up the slips," she remarked, as she nodded in reply to Mona's polite good morning and observed her employment. "I forgot to tell you about the hems last night, and I have been afraid ever since I awoke this morning that you would not make them broad enough."

"Yes, I feared I might make some mistake, so left them," Mona answered, but without stopping her work.

"How beautiful your seams look!" the lady said, as she examined some of the slips. "Your stitches are very fine and even; but over-and-over sewing must be very monotonous work. You might vary it by hemming a sheet now and then. I want the hems three inches wide on both ends."

"Do you have them stitched or done by hand?" Mona inquired.

"Oh, stitched; I have a beautifully running machine, and I want to get them out of the way as soon as possible, for there is dressmaking to be done. Can you run a White machine?"

Mona was conscious that her companion was regarding her

very earnestly during this conversation, but she appeared not to notice it, and replied:

"I never have, but if I could be shown how to thread it, I think I should have no difficulty."

She was very thankful to know that all that mountain before her was not to be done by hand.

"Do you like to sew?" Mrs. Montague inquired, as she watched the girl's pretty hand in its deft manipulation of the needle.

Mona smiled sadly.

"I used to think I did," she said, after a moment's hesitation, "but when one is obliged to do one thing continually it becomes monotonous and irksome."

"How long have you been obliged to support yourself by sewing?" the woman asked, curiously, for to her there seemed to be something very incongruous in this beautiful high-bred girl drudging all day long as a seamstress.

Mona flushed at the question.

There was nothing she dreaded so much as being questioned regarding her past life.

"Not very long; death robbed me of friends and home, and so I was obliged to earn my living," she returned, after considering a moment how she should answer.

"Then you are an orphan?"

"Yes."

"Have you no relatives?" and the lovely but keen blue eyes of the lady were fixed very searchingly upon the fair young face.

"None that I know of."

"You do not look as if you had ever done much work of any kind," Mrs. Montague observed. "You seem more like a person who has been reared in luxury; your hands are very fair and delicate; your dress is of very fine and expensive material, and—why, there is real Valenciennes lace on your pocket-handkerchief!"

Mona was becoming very nervous under this close inspection. She saw that Mrs. Montague was curious about her, though she did not for a moment imagine that she could have the slightest suspicion regarding her identity; yet she feared that she might be trapped into betraying something in an unguarded moment, if she continued this kind of examination.

"I always buy good material," she quietly remarked, "I think it is economy to do so, and—my handkerchief was given to me. How wide did you tell me to make the hems on these pillow-slips?" she asked, in conclusion, to change the subject, but mentally resolving that Mrs. Montague should never see any but plain handkerchiefs about her again.

"I did not tell you any width for the slips," was the dry, yet haughty rejoinder, for madame could not fail to understand that she had been politely admonished that her curiosity was becoming annoying to her fair seamstress, "but you may make them to match those upon the sheets—three inches."

She arose, immediately after giving this order, and swept proudly from the room, and Mona did not see her again that day. It seemed to the poor girl, with her unaccustomed work, the longest one she had ever known, and she grew heavy-hearted, and very weary before it was over.

She had all her life been in the habit of taking plenty of exercise in the open air. While she was studying, Mr. Dinsmore had made her walk to and from school, then after lunch they would either go for a drive or for a canter in the park or the suburbs of the city.

She had never been subjected to any irksome restraint, and so it seemed very hard to be obliged to sit still for so many hours at a time and do nothing but "stitch! stitch! stitch!" like the woman in the "Song of the Shirt."

But six o'clock came at last, to release her from those endless seams and hems, and after she had eaten her dinner she was so completely wearied out that she crept up to her bed and almost immediately fell asleep.

But the next morning she was pale and heavy-eyed, and Mrs. Montague evidently realized that it was unwise to make her apply herself so steadily, for she made out a memorandum of several little things which she wanted and sent Mona down town to purchase them.

The girl came back looking so bright and fresh, and went at her work with so much vigor, the woman smiled wisely to herself.

"She hasn't been used to such close application, it is plain to be seen," she mused, "and I must take care or she will give out. She sews beautifully, though, and rapidly, and I want to keep her, for I believe she can be made very useful."

So every day after that she sent her out for a while on some pretext or other, and Mona felt grateful for these moments of respite.

One day she was sent to Macy's with a longer list than usual, and while there she came face to face with a couple of acquaintances—young ladies who, like herself, had only that winter been introduced to society.

They had been only too eager, whenever they had met her in company, to claim the wealthy Mr. Dinsmore's niece as their friend.

Mona bowed and smiled to-day, as she met them, but was astonished and dismayed beyond measure when they both gave her a rude stare of surprise, and then passed on without betraying the slightest sign of recognition.

For a moment Mona's face was like a scarlet flame, then all her color as quickly fled, leaving her ghastly white as she realized that she had received the cut direct.

Her heart beat so heavily that she was oppressed by a feeling almost of suffocation, and was obliged to stop and lean against a pillar for a moment for support.

She did not see that a young man was standing near, watching her with a peculiar smile on his bold face. He had observed the whole proceeding, and well understood its meaning, while, during all the time that Mona remained in the store, he followed her at a distance. Her emotion passed after a moment, and then all her pride arose in arms. Her eyes flashed, her lips curled, and she straightened herself haughtily.

"They are beneath me," she murmured. "Homeless, friend-less as I am to-day, I would not exchange places with them. I am superior to them even in my poverty, for I would not wound the humblest person in the world with such rudeness and ill-breeding."

Yet, in spite of this womanly spirit, in spite of the contempt which she felt for such miserable pride of purse and position, she was deeply wounded and made to realize, as she never yet had done, that Mrs. Richmond Montague's seamstress would henceforth be regarded as a very different person from Miss Mona Montague, the heiress and a petted beauty in society.

She did not care to go out shopping so much after that; but when obliged to do so she avoided as much as possible those places where she would be liable to meet old acquaintances.

She would take her airing after lunch in the quiet streets of the neighborhood, and then return to her tasks in the sewing-room.

She was not quite so lonely after a dressmaker came to do some fitting for Mrs. Montague, for the woman was kind and sociable, and, becoming interested in the beautiful sewing-girl, seemed to try to make the time pass pleasantly to her, and was a great help to her about her work.

Mona often wondered how Mrs. Montague would feel if she should know who she was. Sometimes she was almost inclined to think that she did suspect the truth, for she often found her regarding her with a curious and intent look. It occurred to her that the woman might possibly have known her mother, and noticed her resemblance to her, for Mr. Dinsmore had told her that she looked very much like her.

One day Mona was standing close beside her, while she tried on a fichu which she had been fixing for her to wear that evening, when the woman broke out abruptly, while she scanned her face intently:

"For whom are you in mourning, Ruth?"

Mona did not know just how to reply to this direct question; but after an instant's reflection she said:

"The dearest friend I had in the world. Do you not remember, Mrs. Montague, that I told you I was an orphan? I am utterly friendless."

Mrs. Montague regarded her with a peculiar look for a moment, but she did not pursue the subject, and Mona was greatly relieved.

"If she knew my mother," she told herself, "and has discovered my resemblance to her—if she knew Uncle Walter, and I had told her I was in mourning for him—she would have known at once who I am."

It was very evident that her employer was pleased with her work, for she frequently complimented her upon her neatly finished seams, while the dressmaker asserted that she had seldom had one so young to work with her who was so efficient.

On the whole she was kindly treated; she was in a pleasant and luxurious home, although in the capacity of a servant; her wages were fair, and for the present she felt that she could not do better than to remain where she was, while she experienced a very gratifying feeling of independence in being able to provide for herself.

She had seen Mr. Graves only once since leaving her own home, and then she had met him on the street during one of her daily walks.

He had told her that Mr. Dinsmore's property had all passed into the hands of his wife, although the house had not as yet been disposed of; it had been rented, furnished, to a family for a year. He said he had never met Mrs. Dinsmore; all her business had been transacted through her lawyer, and the woman evidently did not like, for some reason, to appear personally in the settlement of the property.

He kindly inquired how she endured the confinement of her new life, and urged her cordially to come to him whenever she was tired and needed a rest, telling her that she should always be sure of a warm welcome.

A day or two after this meeting with her old friend, and just as she was returning from her usual walk, Mona encountered a young man as she was about to mount the steps leading into Mrs. Montague's residence.

He was dressed in the height of fashion, and might have been regarded as fairly good-looking if he had not been so conceited and self-conscious.

The young girl did not bestow more than a passing glance upon him, supposing him to be some stranger whom she might never meet again.

She ran lightly up the steps, when, what was her surprise to find him following her, and, just as she was on the point of ringing for admittance, he stayed her hand, by remarking, with excessive politeness:

"I have a latch-key, miss—pray allow me to admit you."

Of course, Mona knew then that this young exquisite must be

the nephew of Mrs. Montague, of whom Mary had told her—Mr. Louis Hamblin.

She observed him more closely as she thanked him, and saw that he was apparently about twenty-five years of age, with light-brown hair, blue eyes, and somewhat irregular, yet not unpleasant, features. He was well formed, rather tall, and carried himself with ease, though somewhat proudly.

He was evidently impressed with Mona's appearance, as his look of admiration plainly indicated.

He appeared to regard her as some visitor to see his aunt, for his manner was both respectful and gentlemanly as he opened the door, and then stood aside to allow her to pass in.

Mona bowed in acknowledgment of this courtesy, and, entering, passed directly through the hall and up stairs, greatly to the young man's astonishment.

He gave vent to a low whistle, and exclaimed, under his breath, as he deposited his cane in the stand and drew off his gloves:

"Jove! I imagined her to be some high-toned caller, and she is only some working girl. Really, though, she is as fine a specimen of young womanhood as I have encountered in many a day, and I should like to see more of her. Ah, Aunt Marg," he went on, as Mrs. Montague came sweeping down the stairs, just then, in an elaborate dinner costume, "how fine you look, and I'm on time, you perceive! How about the McKenzie reception to-night?"

"We must go, of course," responded the lady, in a somewhat weary tone, "for Mrs. McKenzie would be offended if we should remain away, though I am really too tired after the

Ashton ball last evening to go out again; besides, I do not like to wear a dress that isn't properly finished; but I shall have to, for the girls cannot possibly do all that needs to be done."

"You are too particular, Aunt Marg. What if every seam isn't bound just as you like it? Your general make-up is always superb. By the way, who was that girl in black who just came in and went up stairs?" the young man concluded, as if it had only just occurred to him to inquire regarding her.

"Oh, that was Ruth Richards, my seamstress; she had just been out on an errand," Mrs. Montague indifferently returned as they passed into the drawing-room.

"Ruth Richards? Pretty name, isn't it?" her companion remarked, "and the girl herself is a stunner—one does not often meet so lovely a seamstress."

Mrs. Montague turned upon him sharply.

"Nonsense, Louis," she said, impatiently; "don't allow your head to be turned by every pretty face that you see. There are plenty of fine-looking girls in our own set, without wasting your admiration upon a poor sewing-girl."

"I never should have imagined that she was a sewing-girl," Mr. Hamblin returned. "I supposed her to be some aristocratic young lady of your acquaintance, who had come for a social call. She carries herself like a young queen; her form is simply perfect, and her face!—well, were I an artist I should love to paint it," he concluded, with unusual enthusiasm.

Mrs. Montague shrugged her graceful shoulders, and curled her red lips scornfully.

"What would Kitty McKenzie say if she could hear you run on like this about a girl who has to work for her living?" she sneered.

"Kitty McKenzie cannot hold a candle to Ruth Richards. Dress her as Kitty rigs herself out and all New York would be raving about her," the young man replied.

"Louis Hamblin, I am all out of patience with you! Kitty would feel highly complimented with your opinion of her charms," cried his aunt, angrily. "But let me tell you," she added, resolutely, "I shall not countenance any fooling with that young lady; you have shown her very marked attention, and she has a right to expect that you have serious intentions. You know that I should be only too glad to have you marry Kitty; she is a sweet girl, to say nothing about her beauty, while the McKenzies are all that could be desired, both as to wealth and position; and the day that Kitty becomes your wife I will match her dowry as a wedding-gift to you."

"Thank you; I know that you are all that is kind and good in your plans for me, Aunt Margie," Louis responded, in a conciliatory tone, "and you need not fear that I am rashly going to throw Kitty over; we are the best of friends, although not acknowledged lovers. I cannot quite make up my mind to propose, for, really, I do not feel like tying myself down just yet.'

"It would be a good thing for you—you have sown wild oats enough, Louis, and it is time that you began to think of settling down in life. If you please me you know that a brilliant future awaits you, for you are my only heir," Mrs. Montague concluded, as she searched his face earnestly.

"My dear Aunt Margie, you well know there is nothing I like to do better than to please you," was the gallant response, and Mrs. Montague believed him, and smoothed her ruffled plumage.

"Nevertheless," Mr. Louis Hamblin remarked later, while smoking his cigar by himself, "I shall try to see more of that pretty seamstress, without regard to the McKenzie expectations. Jove! what eyes she has! and her low 'thank you,' as I let her in, had the most musical sound I've heard in many a day. Stay," he added, with a start, "now I think of it, she must be the same girl to whom those proud upstarts gave the cut direct in Macy's the other day. I thought her face was familiar, and didn't she pull herself together gloriously after it. There's a romance connected with her, I'll bet. She must have been in society, or she could not have known them well enough to salute them as she did. Really, Miss Ruth Richards grows more and more interesting to me."

CHAPTER XI

RAY'S EXPERIENCE

While Mona was plodding her monotonous way among sheets and pillow-slips, table linen and dressmaking, in Mrs. Montague's elegant home, Raymond Palmer was also being subjected to severe discipline, although of a different character.

We left him locked within a padded chamber in the house of Doctor Wesselhoff, who was a noted specialist in the treatment of diseases of the brain and nerves.

It will be remembered that Ray had been hypnotized into a profound slumber, from which he did not awake for many hours.

When at last he did arouse, he was both calmed and refreshed, while he was surprised to find that a small table, on which a tempting lunch was arranged, had been drawn close beside the lounge where he lay.

He was really hungry, and arose and began to partake with relish of the various viands before him, while, at the same time, he looked about the artfully constructed chamber he was in with no small degree of curiosity.

He remembered perfectly all that had occurred from the time he left his father's store in company with the charming Mrs. Vanderbeck until he had been so strangely over-powered with sleep by the influence of those masterful eyes, which had peered at him through an aperture in the wall.

As his mind went back over the strange incidents of the day he began to experience anew great anxiety over the loss of the rare stones which had been so cleverly stolen from him, and also regarding the fate in store for him.

He knew that the diamonds were in his pocket when the carriage stopped before the house, for he had not removed his hand from the package until Mrs. Vanderbeck discovered that her dress had been caught in the door of the carriage.

That very circumstance, he felt sure, was a part of the skillfully executed plot, and he was convinced that the woman must have robbed him during the moment when he had bent forward and tried to extricate it for her; while she must have concealed the package somewhere in the *coupe* while she was apparently trying to pin together the rent in her dress.

Then, as soon as he alighted, how adroitly she had filled his arms with her bundles and kept his attention so engaged that he did not think of the diamonds again, until the gentleman of the house appeared in the room where Mrs. Vanderbeck had left him.

Oh, how negligent he had been! He should not have released his hold upon that package under any circumstances, he told himself; and yet, he argued, if he had been ever so careful he might have been over-powered and the stones taken by violence, if the woman's cunning had failed to accomplish the desired object.

Mrs. Georgie Sheldon

He firmly believed that he was in a den of thieves, and that the man who had come to him in the reception-room and conducted him into that chamber was in league with the beautiful Mrs. Vanderbeck, who had so fascinated him and hoodwinked his father into sending out such costly jewels for examination.

Then his mind reverted to the strange sensations which he had experienced beneath those human eyes after being trapped into the padded chamber, and a shiver of repulsion ran over him. Was he a captive in the hands of, and at the mercy of, a gang of conjurers and mesmerists? The thought was horrible to him. He had courage enough to defend himself in a hand-to-hand encounter, but he felt powerless to contend against such diabolical influences as he had already been subjected to.

While he was pondering these things, he heard the bolt to the door shoot back, and in another moment a strange man entered the room.

Ray started to his feet, and boldly confronted him.

"Who are you?" he haughtily demanded.

"My name is Huff, sir," the man returned, in a calm, respectful tone, "and I have come to see what I can do for you."

"There is but one thing I desire you to do—release me instantly from this wretched place!" Ray responded authoritatively.

"Yes, yes; all in good time. Doctor Wesselhoff will attend to that," Mr. Huff mildly replied.

"Doctor Wesselhoff?" exclaimed Ray, astonished. "I have heard of him. He is the noted brain and nerve specialist, isn't he?"

"Yes, sir."

"And—am I in *his house*?" the young man demanded, his amazement in nowise abated.

"Yes, this is Doctor Wesselhoff's residence."

"That is very strange! I cannot understand!" Ray remarked, deeply perplexed. "Why am I here?"

"You—have not been quite well of late, and you are here for treatment."

"For *treatment*? Do you mean that I am here as a patient of Doctor Wesselhoff?" cried Ray, aghast.

"Yes, sir, for a little while, until you are better."

"Who brought me here? Who made arrangements for my coming here?"

"Your own friends; and really, sir, it would be better if you would accept the situation quietly," said the man, in a conciliatory tone.

Ray began to get excited again at this information, and the more so, that he did not believe it, while the mystery of his situation seemed to deepen.

He had heard of Doctor Wesselhoff, as he had said; he knew that he was regarded as one of the finest brain specialists in the metropolis, if not in the country, and that, as a man, he stood high in the estimation of the public.

This being the case, he certainly would not lend himself to such an outrageous trick as had been practiced upon him that day.

He did not believe what the old man told him—he did not believe that he was in Doctor Wesselhoff's house at all. It was only a lie on the part of the diamond thieves to further their own schemes, he thought, and yet the man's manner was so respectful, and even kind, that he was deeply perplexed.

"There is nothing the matter with me—I am as sane as you are," he said, flushing angrily at the idea of being regarded as a lunatic.

"Yes—yes; we will hope so," was the gentle response, as the attendant began to gather the dishes and remnants of Ray's lunch.

"You say that my friends brought me here," persisted the young man; "that is false; I was brought here by a woman whom I never saw before, and who robbed me of valuable diamonds. If she arranged for my coming, it is all a trick. But what did she claim was my special malady?" he concluded, with considerable curiosity.

"We will not talk any more about it now, sir, if you please," said his companion, in a soothing tone. "Doctor Wesselhoff will explain it all to you when he returns."

"When he returns? Where has he gone—how long will he be absent?" Ray demanded, with a sinking heart, for time was precious, and he was almost wild to get away to hunt for the thieves who had robbed him; while, too, he knew that his father must already have become alarmed at his long absence.

"The doctor was called away by a telegram only an hour ago," the attendant replied, hoping by this explanation to divert the mind of his charge from his mania of robbery. "His wife, who went South a week ago to visit friends, has been taken suddenly ill, and he was obliged to hasten to her; but he will return at the earliest possible moment."

"Gone *South*! and I must remain here until his return?" Ray cried, in a voice of agony. "I *will* not," he went on fiercely, his face growing crimson with angry excitement. "I tell you I am perfectly well, and I have been only tricked into this place by some cunning thief who has robbed me. Whether Doctor Wesselhoff is concerned in it or not, I cannot tell. I confess it seems very like it to me, although I have always heard him well spoken of. Stay!" he cried, with a start, "you tell me the doctor has already left the city! oh! then he must be a party to the foul wrong of which I am the victim. Let me out—I tell you I *will* not submit to such inhuman treatment," and he turned fiercely upon the attendant, as if he meditated attacking and overpowering him, with the hope of forcing his way from the place.

But the attendant quietly retreated before him, looking him calmly in the eye, and, as Ray pressed closely upon him, he made a few passes before his face with his hands.

Instantly the young man began to experience that same sense of weariness and drowsiness that had over-powered him when those masterful eyes had fastened themselves upon him through the hole in the wall.

"Don't! don't!" he cried, throwing out his arms as if to ward off the influence, while he tried to resist it with all his will-power.

But his arm fell powerless by his side and he sank into a chair near which he was standing, and the attendant turned and left the room, a smile of peculiar satisfaction on his face.

"That was very well done, I think, for a pupil of the great Doctor Wesselhoff," he muttered, as he shot the bolt into the socket and turned to go about other duties. "It will not be long before I shall be able to exert the power as skillfully as he does."

Ray sat as one half dazed for a few moments after the departure of Mr. Huff, and tried to combat with all the strength of his will the strange desire to sleep.

Then suddenly his glance became riveted upon something that was clinging to the leg of his trousers.

He stooped to pick it off, examining it closely, and uttered an exclamation of surprise upon finding that it was a small piece of ladies' cloth of a delicate mauve color.

"Ha!" he cried, excitedly; "it is as precious as gold dust, and may prove to be very useful to me. How fortunate I am to have found it!"

It was a small piece of woolen goods that had been torn from Mrs. Vanderbeck's dress, and Ray, after a moment, put it carefully away in his pocket-book, in the hope of some time finding the rent that it would fit.

It was true that Doctor Wesselhoff had been suddenly called away to his sick wife.

No other summons would have had the power to draw him

away from New York at that time, for he experienced great anxiety and interest regarding the new and peculiar case that had just been confided to his care.

He really believed that Ray—or young Walton, as he believed his patient's name to be, in spite of the fact that he had given it as Palmer—was a monomaniac; for his words and manner fully corroborated the statement which his visitor of the previous day had made to him. He had not the slightest suspicion that he also was the dupe of a cunning plot to secure diamonds that were worth a large sum of money.

But before leaving the city he gave the most careful directions to his pupil, Doctor Huff, who had been studying with him for more than a year, regarding the treatment of his patient, and then he was obliged to hurry away, promising, however, that he would return just as soon as it would do to leave his wife.

It took him two days of continuous travel to reach his destination, and then he found Mrs. Wesselhoff so very ill that all his thought and care were concentrated upon her.

The place to which he went was a remote Southern town, where Northern newspapers seldom found their way; consequently he could not know anything of the intense excitement that was prevailing in New York over the mysterious disappearance of Raymond Palmer and the costly stones he had taken with him.

To his pupil he had hastily explained all that he could regarding the young man's case, and had told him that his name was Walton; so, of course, Doctor Huff, on reading an account of the diamond robbery and the strange disappearance of the merchant's son, never dreamed that the patient left in his charge was the missing young man.

Mr. Palmer did not seem to be at all troubled over the non-appearance of his son until the time arrived to close the store for the night; then he began to feel some anxiety.

Still, he told himself, Ray might possibly have been detained longer than he had anticipated, and finding it rather late to return to the store, had gone immediately home, where there was also a safe in which the diamonds could be deposited for the night.

With this hope to rest upon, he hastened to his residence, but was made even more anxious upon being told by the housekeeper "that Mr. Raymond had not come in yet."

He kept hoping he might come, so he ate his supper and then tried to compose himself to read his papers; but his uneasiness only continued to increase.

He endured the suspense until nine o'clock, and then went down town to consult with the superintendent of police.

He confided to him what had occurred, and his fears regarding the safety of his son, and he was by no means reassured when that official at once exclaimed that "the whole thing was a put-up job."

"Keep quiet," he advised, "for a day or two, and we will see what we can do."

He set his detectives at work upon the case immediately, while the anxious father endeavored to endure his suffering in silence. But the "day or two" brought no revelations, and his agony could no longer be controlled; he believed that his son had been murdered for the sake of the diamonds, and thus the matter became public.

The newspapers were full of the affair, and caused great excitement. The city offered a large reward for any intelligence regarding the missing young man or the diamonds, and this was doubled by Mr. Palmer himself.

But days and weeks passed, and no clew was obtained regarding either the stolen jewels or Ray's mysterious fate; therefore the belief that he had been foully dealt with prevailed very generally.

Mr. Palmer had placed in the hands of a private detective a detailed account in writing of the woman's visit to the store, and also a minute description of herself, and the moment he had finished reading it the man's face lighted up with eager interest, even enthusiasm.

"Great Scott!" exclaimed the detective, with a resounding slap upon his knee, "I'll wager my badge that it's a sequel to that Bently affair, when a young broker of Chicago was wretchedly fooled with some diamonds about three years ago!—that woman also had short, curly red hair."

He related the story to Mr. Palmer, and informed him that he had been engaged upon the case, off and on, for a long time; but since he had come to New York to reside he had about given it up as hopeless.

"This may put me on the trail again, however," finally remarked Mr. Rider, who was the detective that Justin Cutler had employed.

Of course, the house which Mrs. Vanderbeck had given as her place of residence was visited, but as in the Bently affair, it proved to be empty, and Mrs. Vanderbeck seemed to have vanished as completely as if she had been a visitant from some other sphere.

All this had occurred while Mona was so absorbed in her grief for her uncle; when she had had no interest in anything outside her home, and so not having read any of the newspapers, she was entirely ignorant of the excitement that had prevailed over the robbery, and Ray's disappearance. Thus she believed that he had deserted her, like most of her other fair-weather friends, and was trying to make herself believe that he was unworthy of her regard.

Poor Ray! it had fared hard with him during all this time, although not in the way that his father and the detectives feared.

We last saw him just after he had discovered the shred that had been torn from Mrs. Vanderbeck's dress; but when Doctor Huff again went to him he found him prostrate upon the floor in a high fever and delirious.

For four weeks he lay thus. He had taken a severe cold, and that, with the excitement and anxiety caused by the loss of the diamonds, had brought on the illness.

When Doctor Wesselhoff returned after a hard fight with disease in his wife's case, he found him very low, and just at the turning point in his fever.

He bestowed great commendation upon his pupil, however, for his management of the case, which, he said, he could not have treated better himself.

He expressed himself as very much surprised, because none of the young man's friends had called to make any inquiries about him; it certainly showed a lack of interest, if not a positive neglect, he thought.

He believed that the fever would turn favorably, for the young man had a naturally vigorous constitution, and he had known of persons recovering who had possessed far less vitality.

Ray did pass the crisis successfully, but he was very weak for many days longer; too weak even to notice where he was, or who was caring for him.

But, as he gained a little strength, he looked curiously about him, then memory began to assert itself—he recalled the events which had occurred on that fateful day, when he had been made a captive, and he realized that he had been moved from that dismal padded chamber to a large and airy room in another portion of the house.

The next time Doctor Wesselhoff came to his bedside, after he had come thoroughly to himself, he said, in a grave but authoritative voice:

"Doctor Wesselhoff, sit down if you please; I want to talk with you for a few moments."

The physician obeyed, but with some surprise, for both the look and manner of his patient convinced him that he was perfectly rational.

"I have been very ill, have I not?" Ray inquired.

"Yes, but you are much better and steadily improving."

"How long have I been sick?"

"It is more than five weeks now since you were attacked."

Ray frowned at this information.

How must his father feel regarding his strange absence? What had become of that cunning thief and the diamonds? were questions which suggested themselves to him.

But he simply asked:

"When did you return to New York?"

"About a week ago," the physician replied. "I was very sorry to have to leave you as I did, but the summons to my wife was imperative, and of course my duty was by her side."

A sarcastic smile curled Ray's lips at this last remark.

"I am only surprised that you returned at all," he quietly responded.

"Why?" inquired the physician, with some astonishment.

"It is not always safe, you know," Ray answered, looking him straight in the eye, "for one who has aided and abetted a stupendous robbery to appear so soon upon the scene of his depredations."

Doctor Wesselhoff's face fell.

He had hoped that, when the young man should recover, all signs of his peculiar mania would disappear; but this did not seem much like it, and he began to fear the case might prove a very obstinate one.

"I think you must rest now," he remarked, evading the subject; "you have talked long enough this time."

"Perhaps I have, but I do not intend to rest until I have come to some definite understanding regarding my relations with you," Ray responded, resolutely.

"Well, then, what do you mean by a definite understanding?" the physician asked, thinking it might be as well to humor him a little.

"I want to know how far you are concerned in this plot to keep me a prisoner here? I want to know in what way you are connected with that woman who called herself Mrs. Vanderbeck, and who enticed me here with valuable diamonds, only to steal them from me? I believe I am in the power of a gang of thieves, and though I cannot reconcile it with what I had heard of you previously, that you must be associated in some way with them."

Ray had spoken rapidly, and with an air and tone of stern command, which puzzled while it impressed the doctor.

"You bring a very serious charge against me, my young friend," he gravely remarked, but without betraying the slightest resentment; "but perhaps if you will tell me your side of the story I shall understand you better, and then I will explain my authority for detaining you here."

Doctor Wesselhoff was strangely attracted toward his patient. He did not seem at all like an insane person, except upon that one subject, and he would not have regarded that as a mania if he had not been assured of it by Mrs. Walton. He began to think there might at least be some misunderstanding, and that it would be as well to let the young man exhaust the subject once for all; then he could judge the better regarding the treatment he needed.

"Well, then, to begin at the beginning," Ray resumed. "A

woman, giving her name as Mrs. William Vanderbeck, called at my father's store on the day I came here, and asked to look at diamonds. You will remember, I told you my father is a diamond dealer. They were shown to her, and she selected several very expensive ornaments, which she said she wished to wear at a reception that evening. But she represented that she could not purchase them unless they were first submitted to her husband for examination and his sanction. He was an invalid; he could not come to the store, consequently the stones must be taken to him; was there not some reliable person who could be sent to her residence with them, when, if Mr. Vanderbeck was satisfied with the ornaments, a check for their price would be filled out and returned to my father. This seemed fair and reasonable, and I was commissioned to attend the lady and take charge of the diamonds. I put the package in my pocket, and my hand never left it until the *coupe* stopped before this house, when Mrs. Vanderbeck suddenly discovered that her dress had caught in the carriage door, and she could not rise. Of course I offered assistance in disengaging it; but in spite of our united efforts, the garment was torn during the operation. I suppose she robbed me at that moment, but am not quite sure, as I did not discover my loss until you—whom I supposed to be the lady's husband—entered the room, and I slipped my hand into my pocket for the diamonds, only to find that they were gone. You know the rest, and the treatment I received from yourself. Is it any wonder that I believed you an accomplice when I found myself in that padded chamber and losing all sense and reason beneath the influence of a powerful mesmerist?"

Doctor Wesselhoff had listened gravely throughout the young man's recital, and, though astonished and puzzled by what he heard, felt that he was relating a very connected story.

He was upon the point of replying to his questions, when he chanced to glance at his assistant, Doctor Huff, who had been in the room all the time, and saw that he was startlingly pale, and laboring under extreme agitation.

"Sir," cried the man, hoarsely, "can it be possible that he is the victim of the recent diamond robbery, which has created so much excitement? The newspapers have been full of the story that he has just related."

Mrs. Georgie Sheldon

CHAPTER XII

AMOS PALMER FINDS HIS SON

"What do you mean?" Doctor Wesselhoff sharply demanded, and losing color himself at the sudden suspicion that he also might have been the dupe of a set of rogues.

"Haven't you seen an account of the affair in the papers?" Doctor Huff asked. "They were full of it for two weeks after you left home."

"No, I did not see a New York paper from the time I started until I returned. I could not get one, even if I had not had too many cares and been too much absorbed in my wife's critical condition to think of or read news of any kind," Doctor Wesselhoff replied. Then, with a sudden thought, as he turned again to Ray: "Young man, is not your name Walton?"

"You know it is not," said Ray, with a flash of indignation "I told you, the day I came, that my name is Palmer—Raymond Palmer."

"He is the man!" cried the assistant, starting up and regarding the invalid with a look of fear, "and it was Amos Palmer, the diamond merchant, who was robbed!"

"Can it be possible!" exclaimed the physician, amazed at this intelligence. "That woman—Mrs. Walton—told me that he was her son, only at times he denied his own name, so when he told me his name was 'Palmer' that day I imagined it only a freak produced by his mania."

Ray had been regarding the man curiously during this speech. He surely did not appear like a person who would have anything to do with so daring a crime as that of which he had accused him. He was strikingly noble in appearance; his manner was quietly dignified and self-possessed—he had a finely shaped head, a kind eye, a genial smile, while his astonishment and dismay over what he had just been told seemed too genuine to be feigned.

"Did you not expect to find me in your reception-room? Did no lady inform you of my arrival on the day I came here?" Ray inquired, searching his face earnestly.

"No, I saw no lady—a servant came to tell me that a gentleman was waiting to see me," responded the doctor.

"Then she must have gone immediately out and made off with all possible speed," said Ray, musingly.

"But," Doctor Wesselhoff continued, as if he had not heard his remark, "the woman I spoke of—a Mrs. Walton—called upon me the previous day and arranged with me to take you as a patient. She was upward of fifty years of age, her hair was white, and she had the look of one who had known much care and sorrow."

He then proceeded to relate all that had occurred during the interview, and Ray was astonished at the daring scheme which had been so successfully planned and carried out.

When the physician concluded his account, Ray gravely and positively declared:

"I do not know any person by the name of Walton. If this woman told you that she was my mother, she uttered a falsehood, for I have no mother—she died more than ten years ago, and her place has been filled, as well as another could fill it, by a housekeeper. My home is No. 119—street; but, Doctor Wesselhoff, if you still doubt my statements, and imagine that I am laboring under a peculiar mania, you can easily ascertain the truth by bringing my father here to prove my assertions. I beg that you will do so without delay, for he must be suffering the most harrowing suspense on my account."

Doctor Wesselhoff looked very much disturbed, for the more he talked with Ray, the more fully convinced he was that he had been unconsciously lending his aid to further an atrocious crime.

But as he saw how pale and weary his patient was, he was recalled to a sense of his duty as a physician.

He arose and kindly took the young man's hand.

"I am very much afraid," he said, "that we are both the victims of a complicated plot; but let me assure you that so far as I am concerned, the wrong to you shall be made right without a moment's delay. Now I want you to go to sleep, and while you are resting I will seek an interview with the man whom you claim as your father."

Ray's weak fingers closed over the hand he held in a friendly clasp at this assurance, and he was at once inspired with implicit confidence in the physician.

"Thank you," he said, a trustful smile wreathing his thin lips, "I will be obedient and go to sleep, but I shall expect to find my father here when I awake."

"If Amos Palmer is your father, you will surely find him by your bedside after you have had your nap," Doctor Wesselhoff responded, and with another hand-clasp he withdrew from the room.

In less than five minutes Ray was sleeping quietly and restfully.

Half an hour later the great brain specialist rang the bell of Amos Palmer's handsome residence. The servant who answered it replied in the affirmative when asked if the gentleman of the house was in, and ushered the visitor into a richly furnished reception-room leading from the hall.

A few minutes later a sorrowful, despondent-looking gentleman entered, and politely, although somewhat absently, saluted his caller.

He did not look much like the upright, energetic and affable gentleman who had so courteously served the elegant Mrs. Vanderbeck a few weeks previous.

His face was wan and drawn with anguish, his cheeks were hollow, his eyes sunken, heavy and lusterless; his form was bowed, his steps feeble and faltering.

After saluting Doctor Wesselhoff, he threw himself, with a heavy sigh, into a chair, where he immediately became absorbed in his own painful thoughts, appearing to forget that there was any one present, or that there were duties devolving upon him as host.

"Mr. Palmer," said the physician, breaking in upon his sorrowful reverie, "my name is Wesselhoff, and I have called to consult with you regarding the very peculiar circumstances connected with your son's disappearance."

Amos Palmer was like one electrified upon hearing this. He sat erect, and stared with wondering eyes at his companion, and began to tremble violently.

"My son! my son!" he cried, in quavering tones. "Oh, if you can tell me *anything*—if you can tell me that he—lives," the word was scarcely audible, "you will put new life into me."

"Tell me his full name, if you please," said Doctor Wesselhoff, who was scarcely less excited than the trembling man before him.

"Raymond Palmer."

"Describe him to me."

Amos Palmer gave him a minute description of the young man as he appeared on the day that he had been trapped into the physician's house, even to the clothing which he had worn, and the doctor was at last convinced that, all unwittingly, he had assisted in the perpetration of a double crime.

"Yes," he said, when the eager father had concluded, and feeling that he must at once relieve the terrible suspense under which his companion was laboring; "your son lives, and is longing to see his father."

"Oh, then, I have nothing more to wish for—the world will be bright to me once more, for he was my all, Doctor Wesselhoff—my last, and best beloved. I have laid six children in the grave, and all my hopes were centered in Ray. My boy! my boy! I am content to know that you live—that you are not lost to me!"

The over-wrought man broke down utterly at this point, bowed his face upon his hands, and sobbed almost convulsively.

Doctor Wesselhoff was also greatly moved at the sight of his emotion, but as soon as he could control himself sufficiently, he remarked:

"I have a very strange story to tell you, Mr. Palmer, and you may be inclined, as your son was at first, to suspect me of complicity in the affair. I am, however, willing to be subjected to a rigorous investigation, if you demand it; but let me assure you that the moment I discovered the truth, I saw that I, as well as you, had been wretchedly imposed upon, and I was anxious to do all in my power to right the wrong."

He then related all that he had told Ray, and all that we already know, while Amos Palmer listened with wonder to the unfolding of the bold and cunning scheme which had so baffled the police and the best detectives in New York.

"It is the most devilish plot I ever heard of if you will excuse the expression," Mr. Palmer excitedly exclaimed, when his visitor had concluded his narrative.

"It certainly was a very brazen one, yet very cleverly arranged, and just as artfully carried out," Doctor Wesselhoff remarked; and then he inquired, while he regarded his companion with earnest interest: "But have you no doubts as to the truth of my statements? Have you no suspicions that I might also be concerned in the plot?"

Mrs. Georgie Sheldon

"No, sir; I am impressed that you are a man of truth and honor. I have heard of you, and know something of your reputation; and I can but feel thankful that my son fell into your hands, rather than into the clutches of some unprincipled villain," Mr. Palmer replied, with a hearty confidence in his tones that could not be doubted. Then he added: "Excuse me for a few moments while I order my carriage, then you shall take me at once to my son."

Amos Palmer seemed a changed man now that hope throbbed once more in his heart, and he started up with all his old-time vigor and energy to leave the room.

But Doctor Wesselhoff stopped him.

"My own carriage is at your door—do not wait for yours; come at once with me and I will have you sent home when you are ready to return; but Mr. Palmer, you must be prepared to find your son greatly changed, for he has been very ill; the worst is over, however, and he will gain rapidly now, if we take proper care of him."

In a few moments the two men were driving rapidly toward the physician's residence, while they more fully discussed the affair of the robbery, and the skillful way in which it had been managed.

"I would never have believed that a woman could have nerve enough to attempt anything so daring," Mr. Palmer remarked. "I should have been willing to take my oath that she—this Mrs. Vanderbeck, so called—was just what she pretended to be—a refined and cultured lady accustomed to the most polished society. She did not overdo her part in the least, and had one of the most frank and beautiful faces that I have ever seen. Her figure and carriage were superb, her manner charming. The only peculiar thing about her was her hair, which was a decided red, as were also her eyebrows, and lashes. She had fine teeth, and she was very richly, though modestly, dressed. She came to the store apparently in her own carriage, with a colored driver, and everything seemed to indicate that she belonged in the ranks of high life."

"The woman who came to me, to make arrangements for the treatment of her pretended son, was a much older woman than you describe," Doctor Wesselhoff said, in reply, "her hair was almost white, her face was somewhat wrinkled, and she appeared sad and depressed. It must be that there were two women concerned in the affair, for my visitor remarked that since her son, when under the influence of his mania, was so determined to have her arrested, she would send her sister, whom she called Mrs. Vanderbeck, with him."

"Hum—maybe my adventuress was the same person in disguise," Mr. Palmer thoughtfully observed.

"But you said she had red hair, brows, and lashes, and was quite young in appearance; while Mrs. Walton was old and wrinkled, with white hair; the brows and lashes I did not notice particularly, but they certainly were not red," Doctor Wesselhoff responded, doubtfully.

"Well, whether they were one and the same or not, the whole thing is a perplexing puzzle, and I would sacrifice a good deal to have it solved," said Mr. Palmer. "But," he added, with a sigh, "I am afraid that it never will be, for the thieves, in all probability, left New York immediately, and were sharp enough to remove the diamonds from their settings before attempting to dispose of them."

"They may overreach themselves yet and be brought to justice," Doctor Wesselhoff remarked. "But is there no way of identifying the diamonds unset?"

"Some of them—two in particular—could be identified; they were a pair of magnificent solitaires, and I am sure my expert could tell them anywhere," Mr. Palmer replied.

"It is strange that you were not suspicious of a person who wished to purchase so many diamonds at one time," said the physician, thoughtfully.

"She did not pretend that she wished to buy all that she laid out, only that her selections from the lot were to be made with the advice and sanction of her husband; and in this way—don't you see?—the clever sharper got possession of a great deal more than she would otherwise have done."

"True, she showed herself very shrewd. But your son has in his possession a clew, though a very slender one, which may possibly lead to a solution of the mystery. It is a small piece of cloth that was torn from the woman's dress," Doctor Wesselhoff returned.

"I am afraid that won't amount to much, for, probably, if the woman is still in New York, which I doubt, she will never wear that dress again," Mr. Palmer responded. "But," he continued, cheerfully, "I shall not complain as long as I am to have Ray back again. I fully believed that he had been murdered. My loss I can never tell you what anguish I have endured, for will of course eat deeply into the profits of my business for this year, but that is of comparatively little consequence. I am more troubled to have such wickedness prosper than I am about any pecuniary loss."

The carriage stopped just then, and the conversation ended. Both gentlemen alighted, and Doctor Wesselhoff led the way into his house, and straight up to the chamber which

Ray occupied.

He had not aroused once during the doctor's absence, but awoke almost immediately after their entrance, and the meeting between the father and son was both joyful and tender.

Neither had ever before realized how much they were to each other, or believed that life could be so dark if they were separated.

Doctor Wesselhoff would not allow them to talk very much that night, for he said that his patient was liable to have a relapse if he became too weary or was subjected to too much excitement; so Mr. Palmer was permitted to remain only a short time with him, but promised to return again at as early an hour in the morning as the physician would allow.

He visited Ray twice every day after that, and both father and son were fully convinced of the truth and honesty of purpose of the noted specialist, who had given Ray such excellent care, and whose interest in him continued to increase throughout his recovery.

The Palmers found him very genial and entertaining, and an enduring friendship grew up between the three.

Ray improved very rapidly, and was able by the end of two weeks to return to his own home; but, though he was very thankful to be restored to health and to his father once more he was saddened and dismayed upon learning of Mr. Dinsmore's sudden death, and that Mona had been deprived of her inheritance.

He was still more appalled when, upon making inquiries, he could learn nothing of her movements since leaving her home. No one seemed to know anything about her—even her friend Susie Leades was in ignorance of her whereabouts, for Mona had shrunk, with extreme sensitiveness, from telling any one, save Mr. Graves, of her plans for the future.

Ray did not know who had been Mr. Dinsmore's man of business, so, of course, he could not appeal to the lawyer, and he was finally forced to believe that Mona had left New York.

He could not be reconciled to have her vanish so completely out of his life, just when he had begun to entertain such strong hopes of winning her for his wife.

For more than two years he had loved Mona Montague in secret, but only during the last few months had he allowed himself to show her marked attention.

She had been in school until the previous June, and he had felt sure that Mr. Dinsmore would not countenance anything that would distract her mind from her studies, therefore he had waited, with commendable patience, until she graduated before making it manifest that he experienced any especial pleasure in her society.

Mr. Dinsmore and Mona had spent the months of July and August at Lenox, Massachusetts, and Ray, having learned their plans, arranged to be there at the same time. Therefore the young people had seen considerable of each other during the summer, and before their return to New York, Ray Palmer had begun to have strong hopes that he should eventually win the beautiful girl for his wife.

They met several times in society during the early winter, and Mona always appeared so happy with him that he gradually grew bolder in his attentions, and finally formally requested the pleasure of acting as her escort in public. This request was granted, as we know, and cordial permission to call was also given him, and when Ray left Mona that night, after their attendance at the opera, he resolved to seek Mr. Dinsmore at an early day and ask the privilege of paying his addresses to his niece with the view of winning her.

But he was very unhappy over his fruitless efforts to find her, and he grew strangely silent and depressed, greatly to his father's surprise, even while he was every day gaining in health and strength.

Finally Mr. Palmer questioned him outright as to the cause; and Ray, longing for both sympathy and advice, frankly told him the truth.

"That is too bad, Ray, and I am extremely sorry," the royal-hearted man remarked. "I should be very sorry to have you disappointed in such a matter, but do not be discouraged; we will do our best to find the young lady, and then you shall bring her home as soon as you please."

"Then you approve of my choice?" Ray remarked, with some surprise at his father's interest and even anxiety to have him succeed in his suit.

"Why not? I do not know Miss Montague, but I am sure that a niece of Mr. Dinsmore, and reared with the care which he would be likely to bestow upon her, could be objectionable to no one. Mr. Dinsmore was one of the noblest of men," said Mr. Palmer, with hearty commendation.

"But Mona is only a penniless girl now," Ray responded, determined that his father should fully comprehend the situation. "Mr. Dinsmore's wife has claimed all his property, I have been told, and even if I could find and win her, my bride would have to come to me without any dowry."

"That wouldn't trouble me in the least, my boy, provided the girl herself was all right," his father gravely returned. "We have enough,' he continued, smiling, "without desiring to enrich ourselves by marrying money. You shall choose your own wife, Ray, be she rich or poor, plain or beautiful; only find a sensible little woman who will be a true wife and make you happy, and I shall be more than satisfied."

"Thank you, father," Ray gratefully returned. "I wish there were more men like yourself in the world—there would surely be fewer ill-assorted marriages if there were. Only let me find Mona, and I will soon convince you that she will be a girl after your own heart, as well as mine."

CHAPTER XIII

AT THE RECEPTION

One evening, after Ray's entire restoration to health, he and his father attended a reception given by an old friend of Mr. Palmer's.

It was an unusually brilliant affair, for the Merrills were wealthy people, and very socially inclined, and many of the best people of New York were present.

Mr. Palmer was conversing with his host in a quiet way during a few moments while he was at liberty, when his attention was attracted by the entrance of a new arrival, whose advent seemed to create an unusual flutter of interest.

"Who is she?" he inquired, as the lady slowly approached them, smiling, bowing, and responding to the eager greetings on every hand. "She is a magnificent-looking woman."

"She is Mrs. Montague—a wealthy widow, and a great favorite in society," his friend replied, while his own eyes rested admiringly upon the lady.

"Montague! Montague!" Mr. Palmer repeated reflectively, while he said to himself: "That is the name of Ray's little lady-love; perhaps this woman is a relative, and the girl has gone to live with her. I must find out about that." Then, with this thought in view, he added, aloud; "Introduce me, will you, Merrill?"

His host glanced roguishly at him, and a smile of amusement hovered about his lips as he replied:

"Certainly, if you wish, but I give you fair warning that she is a dangerous party, and especially so to widowers—there are a dozen, more or less, who have already had their wings thoroughly singed."

Mr. Palmer smiled with an air of calm superiority.

"Well, Merrill, I admit that she is as fine-looking a woman as I have ever seen," he said, "but I believe that I am proof against the blandishments of the fair sex upon principle; for," more gravely, "I have never had any desire to change my condition since I lost my wife. My reason for requesting the introduction was, I thought Mrs. Montague might be able to give me some information regarding another lady of the same name."

"All right; an introduction you shall have; but pray take heed to my warning, all the same, and look out for yourself," was the laughing rejoinder. "Ah," as he bowed graciously to the lady approaching them, "we are very glad to be favored with your presence this evening, and now allow me to present a friend; Mrs. Montague, Mr. Palmer."

The brilliant woman shot one sweeping glance out of her expressive eyes at the gentleman and then extended her faultlessly gloved hand to him in cordial greeting.

"I am very glad to make Mr. Palmer's acquaintance," she

said, graciously, "although," she added, with a charming smile, "I cannot look upon him quite as a stranger, for I have friends who frequently speak of him, and in a way that has made one wish to know him personally."

Mr. Palmer flushed slightly as he bowed in acknowledgment of such high praise, and remarked that he felt himself greatly honored.

Mrs. Montague then adroitly changed the tenor of the conversation, and kept him chatting some time, before he thought of Mona again, and when he did, he hardly knew how to broach the subject to his companion.

"Have you resided long in New York, Mrs. Montague?" he inquired, after a slight pause in their conversation.

"Only about six months, but, Mr. Palmer, during that time, I have found your city a most delightful one, socially," the lady returned.

"I understand that Mrs. Montague is quite a favorite in society, which accounts, in a measure, perhaps, for her own enjoyment of its people," the gentleman gallantly responded.

Mrs. Montague flushed slightly and lowered her white lids, modestly, for an instant, and Mr. Palmer continued:

"Allow me to ask, Mrs. Montague, if you ever met Mr. Walter Dinsmore?"

"Dinsmore—Dinsmore," repeated his fair companion, with a puzzled expression; "it seems as if I have heard the name, and yet—I am quite sure that I have met no such person since my residence in New York. Let me see," she added, as if suddenly remembering something—"did I not read in the papers, a short time ago, of the death of the gentleman—he was quite a prominent citizen, was he not?"

"Yes, and much respected; he died suddenly, leaving a large fortune. The reason I inquired if you knew him," Mr. Palmer explained, "was because he left a niece whose name is the same as yours, and I thought possibly you might be a relative of the family. Miss Mona Montague is the young lady's name."

"Mona Montague?" repeated Mrs. Montague, burying her face for an instant in the bouquet she carried as if to inhale its perfume. "No, I think not—I have no relatives in New York except a nephew, who is the same as a son to me. We came to your city entire strangers to every one. But how old is this Miss Montague?"

"About eighteen years of age, I believe. She was said to be a very beautiful girl, and every one supposed her to be Mr. Dinsmore's heiress; but it seems that he had a wife living, although he was supposed to be a widower—who claimed everything, and thus Miss Montague was rendered homeless and penniless. She has certainly disappeared from the circle in which she hitherto mingled."

"How exceedingly unfortunate!" murmured Mr. Palmer's fair listener, with apparent sympathy.

"Very," said the gentleman; "and as we—I feel deeply interested in her, I hoped, when I heard your name, that you might prove to be a relative, and could give me some information regarding her."

"I should be most happy to oblige you, Mr. Palmer," Mrs. Montague sweetly returned, "but I have never met the young lady, and I know nothing about her present circumstances. Is she a connection of yours?"

"No, madame—that is, not as yet," Mr. Palmer answered, with a slight twinge of embarrassment. "I knew Mr. Dinsmore, however, and it seems a very sad thing that his niece should be deprived of both home and fortune, as well as her only friend, especially when he was so fond of her and intended that she would inherit his property. I would give a great deal to know where she is; she would not long be without a home if I could find her."

"Does the man want to marry the girl?" was Mrs. Montague's mental query, as she glanced keenly at her companion. "I begin to believe I should like to see this wonderful creature."

"You say she is very beautiful?" she remarked, aloud.

"So I have been told, and very lovely in character, also."

"Then you have never seen her? Surely you are very philanthropic to be so deeply interested in an entire stranger," Mrs. Montague observed. Then, without giving him an opportunity to reply, she asked, abruptly: "Mr. Palmer, who is that lady just entering the room? She is very striking in appearance, and what a profusion of magnificent diamonds she has on her person!"

Mr. Palmer started at this last observation, and turned to look at the new arrival.

He saw a woman of about thirty-five, rather stout in figure, very showily dressed, and wearing a great many exquisite diamonds of great value.

The man's keen eyes went flashing over her with eager scrutiny, his heart beating rapidly, as he asked himself if it might not be possible that some of his own precious gems were among the jewels that she wore.

The suspicion flashed upon him, in spite of the fact that the woman was a guest in the house of his friend, for he knew that thieves had been found mingling with the brilliant throngs attending regular receptions in New York, and might be again.

But of course he could recognize none of them under such circumstances, and his face fell after one sweeping glance.

"It would be impossible to identify any of the stones without a glass, even if they were there," he said to himself; "for, of course, the thief, whoever she was, would have had the stones reset before wearing them anywhere."

"Yes," he said, aloud, "the lady has a fortune upon her person; but I do not know her. Speaking of diamonds," he continued, glancing at the ornaments which Mrs. Montague wore, "you will pardon me, I am sure, if I tell you that you, also, have some very fine stones. I consider myself a connoisseur regarding diamonds and capable of judging."

"Yes," Mrs. Montague quietly responded, "I have some choice ones, and I am very fond of diamonds; but I have never seen any one, unless it was an actress, with such a profusion of them as that lady. I do not think I should care to wear so many at one time, even if I possessed them."

"No, it hardly seems in good taste," Mr. Palmer replied, then added: "My son is beckoning me; will you excuse me for a moment?"

"Your *son*!" exclaimed the lady, with a light laugh and an arch look. "Surely, Mr. Palmer, *you* cannot have a son old enough to mingle in society like this?"

"Indeed I have, and you can see for yourself—he is standing yonder by that large easel," the gentleman returned, laughing also, and evidently well pleased to be regarded younger than he really was.

"I must confess my surprise," said the charming widow, as she darted a curious glance at the young man, "but since you assert it I must not doubt your word, and I will say, also, that you have every reason to be proud of your son. But—I will not detain you," she added, bowing gracefully; "only I trust that I may have the pleasure of meeting you again."

"Thank you, madame; you honor me," the diamond merchant replied, as he, too, bowed, and then passed on.

"Merrill said truly," he muttered, as he made his way through the crowd toward Ray; "she is certainly a very charming woman; I don't wonder that she is a favorite in society. Well, what is it, Ray, my boy?" he asked, as he reached his son's side.

"Did you notice that woman who entered the room a moment or two ago?" the young man asked, in a low tone.

"The one wearing so many diamonds?"

"Yes; and, father, I believe there is some of our property about her."

"I thought of it, too, Ray, but only because she wore so many stones, I suppose. We surely have no right to suspect her of being the thief," said Mr. Palmer, gravely.

"Perhaps not; but I did, all the same."

Mrs. Georgie Sheldon

"She does not look at all like that Mrs. Vanderbeck," Mr. Palmer remarked, as he again singled out the woman, and observed her closely.

"I don't know; her form is not unlike; and put a red wig on her, she might pass—"

"Pshaw, Ray," interrupted his father, "you are letting your imagination run away with you; she cannot be the same person; her features are entirely different, and she is too stout."

"Well, that may be; but I am impressed that some of those stones belong to us," Ray said, following the woman with a critical glance.

"If any of them are ours, we have no means of identifying them," Mr. Palmer responded. "I have given them up as a dead loss, and do not believe that we shall ever discover the thief."

Ray looked very sober.

"I am very sore over that affair, father," he said, gravely. 'If I had not allowed my head to be turned by that fascinating woman, I never should have lost them. She just smiled and talked all the sense out of me. I ought never to have removed my hand from that package, even to prevent a dozen tailor-made dresses from being torn, and then she could not have stolen it."

"Don't grieve over it, Ray, for it will not avail," his father returned, kindly. "Experience is the best teacher, and no one will ever rob us in the same way again."

"I do not think that is likely, and yet I cannot get over it; I cannot bear to consider the gems irretrievably lost, even yet."

"You may as well, for I am sure we shall never see any of them again," said Mr. Palmer, calmly.

"Who is this lady approaching us?" Ray asked, after a moment. "You were talking to her when I motioned to you."

Mr. Palmer glanced up.

"That is a Mrs. Montague—"

"Montague!" interrupted Ray, in a startled tone. "Can she be anything to Mona?"

"No, nothing. I asked the question upon learning her name," his father answered.

Ray sighed heavily; then, as his glance still lingered upon the beautiful woman, he exclaimed:

"Isn't she lovely? I believe she is the purest blonde I have ever seen. Her hair is like spun gold, her features are faultless, and her neck and arms are as perfect as if sculptured from marble."

"Take care, Ray," said his father, with a sly smile; "people say that she is a perfect siren. I have myself been warned against her to-night."

"Pshaw!" retorted the young man. "Where is her husband?"

"She has none, and therein lies the danger."

"Ah! a widow! How old is she?"

"Not more than twenty-eight or thirty, I judge—at least, she does not look it in full dress, and she is very charming in manner. Merrill says that all the men, both old and young, are making fools of themselves over her."

"Well, then, you and I will not help to swell the list," said Ray, curtly, a trifle irritated that his staid and dignified father should have so much to say about the gay society woman; and turning on his heel, he moved away, with the purpose of approaching the one whose diamonds had attracted so much attention. He meant to seek an introduction, and get an opportunity to examine the stones more closely.

Fifteen minutes later he stood bowing before her, as a friend presented him, and he was long in recovering from the shock which went through him as he caught the name by which she was introduced:

"Mrs. Vanderbeck, allow me to present my friend, Mr. Palmer."

"Pardon me. Did I understand the name—Mrs. Vander*beck*?" Ray said, trying to control the rapid throbbing of his pulses, and putting a slight emphasis upon the last syllable of the name.

He was sure that the lady started and changed color as he did so, for he was watching her closely.

"No," she said; "you haven't it quite right; we spell it *h-e-c-k*."

But she seemed strangely ill at ease during the few moments that Ray stood conversing with her, while from time to time he caught her regarding him curiously. He did not, however, get any satisfaction from his examination of her ornaments; for among such a blazing array of diamonds it was impossible to tell if he had ever seen any of them before.

"I believe she was connected in some way with that strange affair. She *may* be the woman who called upon Doctor Wesselhoff to arrange for my imprisonment," he said to himself, after he had left her. "At all events," he added, resolutely, "I am going to lay the matter before Detective Rider, and see what he thinks about it."

He was more strongly confirmed in his suspicions a few minutes later, when he saw Mrs. Vanderheck bidding her host and hostess good-night, and then withdraw from the company.

About ten o'clock supper was served, and, strangely enough, after the company was seated, Ray found that his left-hand neighbor was no other than the fascinating Mrs. Montague, while, glancing beyond her, he saw that his father had acted as her escort to the table.

It annoyed him exceedingly to see them together, and to observe the gallantry with which his father was attending to the fair widow's wants.

During all the years that had elapsed since the death of his mother, Mr. Palmer had not manifested the slightest desire for the society of ladies, and Ray had never thought of such a thing as his marrying again.

But now it suddenly flashed across him: "What if this gay woman of the world, with her beauty and powers of fascination, should tempt him to make her the mistress of his home and wealth?"

The thought was far from agreeable to him, and yet he could not have told why.

He could find no fault with Mrs. Montague personally; she

was beautiful in face and figure; she was delightful in manner. Why, then, did he shrink from the thought of having her come into the family?

Was he jealous? Was he selfish? Did he begrudge his father the comfort and enjoyment of a more perfect domestic life? Was he unwilling to have any one come between them? Was he fearful that his own prospects—his expectations of wealth—would be affected by such a union?

All these questions darted through his mind, and he felt shamed and humiliated by them. He could not analyze his feelings; he only knew that the thought was not pleasant to him.

Mr. Palmer soon espied his son, and leaning back in his chair, asked, with his usual genial smile:

"Well, Ray, who have you for a companion?"

"Miss Grace Merrill," he briefly responded.

"Ah! a pleasant girl; but allow me to make you acquainted with your left-hand neighbor also; Mrs. Montague, my son, Mr. Raymond Palmer."

Mrs. Montague turned to the young man with her most brilliant smile, though a gleam of amusement illuminated her lovely eyes, as she remarked the conscious flush upon the elder gentleman's face, as he performed the ceremony of introduction.

"I am delighted to meet you, Mr. Palmer," she said: "but I could hardly believe that you were the son when your father pointed you out to me.'

Ray could not have been ungracious beneath the charm of her manner, even had he been naturally so, and he soon found himself disarmed of all his disagreeable reflections and basking with delight in the sunshine of her presence, her bright wit and repartee, and her sweet, rippling laugh. By the time supper was over it would have been difficult to tell who was the more ardent admirer of the fascinating widow—the father or the son.

Later in the evening she ran across him again by accident(?), and another half-hour spent in her society completed the glamour which she had thrown around him at supper, and, in spite of his assertion to the contrary, it really seemed as if Raymond Palmer was likely to help swell the "list of fools" who blindly worshiped at her shrine.

Mrs. Georgie Sheldon

CHAPTER XIV

LOUIS HAMBLIN IS INTERESTED IN MONA

Mrs. Richmond Montague had a purpose in honoring Mr. Palmer and his handsome son with so much of her society on the evening of Mr. Merrill's reception.

When Mr. Palmer had mentioned the name of Mona Montague, inquiring if she was a relative of the young girl, a sudden shock had thrilled through her nerves, for it was a name which, for certain reasons, with her whole heart, she *had hated*, although, as she believed, she had never seen the young lady.

Before the evening was over, however, she had learned why the diamond merchant was so anxious to find the ex-heiress of Walter Dinsmore.

She discovered, by adroit references and questions, by putting this and that together, that Ray Palmer was in love with the girl; that the old gentleman favored his suit in spite of her poverty, and would willingly have sanctioned an immediate marriage if she could have been found.

"So much for this evening, and now I wish that I could find the girl," she mused, as she stood before her mirror and removed her ornaments, after returning from the reception. "So she is beautiful! I wonder if she looks like her mother— my hated rival! Ah! Mona Montague, I vowed that I would have vengeance, and I had it. You dared to come between me and the man I loved, and I swore I would crush you—I did, and now I mean to crush your child also, if I can find her. True, I won your husband after you were dead and gone, but he never loved me as he loved you, in spite of my blind idolatry for him."

She had become greatly excited over these reflections, and, sweeping into a heap the laces and jewels which she had removed from her person, she began pacing the floor with swift, angry steps.

"I wish now," she began again, after a time, "that I had gone to Walter Dinsmore's funeral, if for nothing more than to get a glimpse of the girl; but he bore me no good-will, and somehow I could not make up my mind to enter his house. I am sorry I didn't, for then I should have known this pretty little lady-love of Mr. Ray Palmer, if ever I met her again. Now I may have a long hunt for her. It was a great oversight on my part; but I never thought of her disappearing in such a mysterious way."

After a while she removed her rich evening costume, then donning a warm flannel wrapper, she seated herself before the glowing grate, clasped her hands around her knees, and, gazing upon the bed of red-hot coals, she fell to musing.

"So young Palmer is bound to marry Richmond Montague's fair daughter," she murmured, with curling lips and a bitter laugh; "and his father is only too willing, provided she can be found. Ha! ha! ha!" a soft, rippling laugh of intense amusement and scorn bursting from her red lips. "I wonder what they would say if they knew all that I know? I'd give a great deal if I could ascertain just how much the girl knows about herself. She could make a great deal of trouble for me if—"

She broke off suddenly just here, but after a few moments of thought resumed, in another strain:

"I believe I shall have to cultivate my new acquaintances. I think I can play the father against the son, and, *vice versa*, for it was evident to-night that both, with very little encouragement, would become my willing slaves. I imagine that the senior Palmer might make a very agreeable companion. He is reported to be rich—a diamond merchant, and I am fond of diamonds. He is certainly very gallant and not bad-looking. Yes, I think I must cultivate him; and then, if the junior member should discover his inamorata by and by, a word in the ear of the father might be sufficient to blast Miss Mona's hopes, and thus complete the work I began so successfully—at least in some respects—so many years ago. Ah, Madame Mona, you did not realize the strength of the spirit which you defied that day in Paris. I made you *believe* that your marriage was all a sham, but if I could have made it really so I should have been better pleased with my work, for then I should have had nothing to fear, at this late day, from your child."

It is impossible to describe the venom and hatred that were concentrated in the voice of this beautiful woman, as she thus reviewed this portion of her history, which, as can plainly be seen, had left a keen sting in her heart, notwithstanding her boasted victory over her rival.

It did not seem possible that she could be the same person, with her dark, revengeful face, her contracted brow, fiercely gleaming eyes, and that cruel, bitter curl upon her lips, who, in all the glory of her beauty and powers of fascination, had been the centre of attraction in Alexander Merrill's elegant residence less than two hours previous.

It almost seemed as if she must be possessed of a dual nature, similar to that so cleverly represented in the story of "Doctor Jekyll and Mr. Hyde." Then, she had been all smiles, and sweetness, and graciousness, a vision of delight, a presence that charmed and pleased every one with whom she came in contact; now, she was transformed into a beautiful fiend, with a nature of spite and fury, and cruel revenge written upon every delicate feature.

She sat there in the glow of the firelight until the gilded clock on the mantel chimed the hour of two; then, with passion and pain showing themselves in her every movement, she arose, and without undressing, threw herself upon her bed, and wept herself to sleep.

* * * * *

Mona was gradually becoming accustomed to her new life, although it was so very different from the almost charmed existence which she had hitherto led, and had it not been for her grief for her uncle and on account of Ray's seeming neglect and indifference, she would not have been unhappy in her position.

Mrs. Montague was not unreasonable—she did not overwork her, although there was always plenty of sewing to be done. She rather enjoyed being busy, on the whole, while she experienced a great deal of satisfaction in knowing that she could be independent; she even felt something of pride, in thus rising above the adverse circumstances that had so unexpectedly overtaken her.

She was very careful about her health, for she knew that this

Mrs. Georgie Sheldon

sudden change from her previous active care-free life to such sedentary habits, must be a great tax upon her constitution, and so she persisted in taking exercise in the open air every day, although often she would have preferred to remain in the house.

A couple of days after her encounter with Mr. Louis Hamblin upon the steps of Mrs. Montague's residence, she was returning from her usual stroll, when the young man again suddenly appeared around the corner of a street she was passing, and almost ran into her.

"I beg your pardon, Miss Richards," he exclaimed, stopping short, and regarding her with apparent surprise, while he lifted his hat to her with great politeness, "I hope I did not startle you."

"Oh, no; and you are quite excusable," Mona responded, but somewhat astonished that he should address her by her name; but she imagined that he must have asked Mrs. Montague who she was.

She was about to hasten on, when he remarked:

"Since we are both going the same way, perhaps you will allow me to walk with you."

Mona would have preferred to proceed on her way alone, but she had not quite the courage to say so, since he appeared so courteous, so she made no reply at all.

The young man took her silence for consent, and, falling into step with her, began chatting as freely as if they had been old acquaintances.

His manner was very respectful, while there was nothing in

what he said to which she could in the least object—indeed, she found him rather entertaining at first, and almost forgot, for the time, that she was Ruth Richards, the seamstress, instead of Mona Montague, the heiress, and social equal of any high-toned young man whom she might meet.

"Have you lived long in New York, Miss Richards?" Mr. Hamblin inquired, after he had rattled on about various matters, and Mona had hardly spoken. He desired to hear her talk, that he might judge of her mental caliber.

"Yes, thirteen or fourteen years," Mona replied.

Louis Hamblin frowned; he had hoped that she was a stranger there.

"Ah! Then of course New York is very familiar to you," he remarked. "Do your friends reside here?"

"No—I have no friends;" Mona said, flushing and with starting tears.

"Indeed," returned her companion, in a tone of sympathy, "I noticed that you were in mourning—I am very sorry."

Mona had heard so few words of sympathy of late that she came near losing her self-control at this, and she found herself unable to make any reply, lest her tears should fall.

"You look very delicate, too," her companion continued, bending a curious glance upon her. "I am sure you have not always lived as you are living now; it must be very hard to sit and sew all day. I hope you find my aunt considerate, Miss Richards."

Mona was astonished at this last remark which she thought

was in very bad taste, and she turned a cold, questioning glance upon him.

"If at any time you should not," he went on, flippantly, "just let me know, Miss Richards, and I will see what I can do for you, for I have considerable influence with Aunt Marg."

Mona looked amazed, and wondered what he could mean by speaking in such a way of Mrs. Montague.

He had made a grand mistake in assuming that she should make a confidant of him—an entire stranger—in the event of her being overworked by his aunt.

"Mrs. Montague has been very good," she said, icily, and drawing her slight, graceful figure haughtily erect, "but—if at any time I *should* find my duties heavier than I could perform faithfully, I should tell *her* so and seek some other position."

Mr. Hamblin flushed hotly—not with embarrassment, although he had seldom had such a rebuff, but with anger and chagrin that a poor sewing-girl whom he had seen fit to patronize, should dare to give him such a set-back.

But he had no intentions of being beaten at his game, and so curbed his ire for the time.

"Pardon me," he humbly responded, "I did not mean to offend you nor to interfere, 'pon my word I didn't; only you seem so delicate and unfit for such a life; and fashionable ladies have such oceans of work to be done that they sometimes crowd their help—I—"

"Excuse me—I must leave you here; my work is waiting for me," Mona interposed, coldly, and cutting him short as they reached Mrs. Montague's residence.

She ran lightly up the steps and rang the bell before he could offer to admit her with his latch-key as before.

A servant let her in immediately, and she went directly up stairs, without deigning her would-be escort another word or look, while she carried herself with so much hauteur that he knew she resented his presumptuous familiarity.

"Hoity toity!" he muttered, with a crimson face; "our pretty seamstress hath the manner of a princess! One would almost suppose that she had been born and bred in a palace and was the mistress of millions, instead of being only a common working-girl and dependent upon the skill of her own dainty fingers for her living. But she is wonderfully interesting, aside from her beauty, and I must change my tactics or I shall never get into her good graces. Who would have dreamed that she would have the sense to resent my offer. Most girls would have blushed, simpered, and thanked me, feeling flattered with my condescending interest."

Mr. Hamblin did change his tactics.

The next morning, when Mona went into the sewing-room, she found a tiny vase filled with choice flowers upon her table.

She suspected that Mr. Hamblin might have been the donor, and she was annoyed that he should presume to take such a liberty upon so slight an acquaintance. Still, she was not sure that he had put them there, and the pretty things made a bright spot in the room, while their fragrance was not without its charm for her; so she did enjoy them in a measure.

"Where did you get your flowers, Ruth?" Mrs. Montague

inquired, when she came in later to inquire regarding a wrap that was being mended, and espied them.

"My flowers!" Mona said, determined that she would not claim them; "they are not mine, and I do not know who put them here. I found them on the table when I came down this morning."

Mrs. Montague frowned, but said nothing more.

She suspected who had made the floral offering, however, and secretly resolved that Louis should not be guilty of continuing such attentions to her seamstress.

She gave orders to Mary to go into the sewing-room every morning before breakfast, and if she found flowers there to take them down to the dining-room and put them upon the table.

The girl found a bouquet on Mona's table three mornings in succession.

She carried out her mistress' instructions to the letter, and Mr. Louis Hamblin, observing the disposition of his expensive gifts, imagined that the pretty seamstress herself had taken this way to reject them.

The measure angered him, and only made him more resolute to conquer Mona's indifference and pride.

"By Jove!" he said to himself, as he gazed frowningly upon the discarded blossoms, "I believe I am really becoming interested in the proud little beauty, and I must find some other way to bring her around. It is evident that she recognizes the social distance between us, and wishes me to understand it. Perhaps, however, with a little judicious coaxing of a different character, I may win her to a more friendly mood."

He waylaid Mona several times after that, while she was out walking, but, though she never forgot to conduct herself in the most lady-like manner she plainly indicated by her coldness and reserve that she did not care to cultivate Mr. Hamblin's acquaintance.

This opposition to his wishes only made him the more persistent, and added zest to his pursuit of her.

The girl's exquisite beauty and grace—her high-bred self-possession and polished manner—impressed him as he had never been impressed before, even by the society girls whom he was in the habit of meeting, and Kitty McKenzie's charms grew pale and dim beside the brighter and more perfect loveliness of this dainty sewing-girl.

When Mona found that the young man persisted in following her and forcing his society upon her, she changed the time of her daily walk to an hour when she knew he would be down town, and she also took care to go in different directions, thus successfully avoiding him for some time.

But fortune favored him later on.

One morning Mrs. Montague came into the sewing-room all animation, and beaming with smiles.

"Ruth, I am going to ask a great favor of you," she said: "I wonder if you will oblige me."

"Certainly, Mrs. Montague, I shall be very glad to do so, if it is within my power," Mona readily responded.

"Well, then," continued the lady, "I am invited to spend a week at the residence of a friend who lives near Rhinebeck, a little way up the Hudson. Quite a party are going also, and great preparations have been made for us. In fact, it is to be a sort of carnival, on a small scale, and is to wind up with a grand ball. Now, I want you to go with me, Ruth, to help arrange my different costumes, and to act as a kind of dressing-maid—you have such good taste and judgment. Will you go? You will, of course, be relieved from your regular work, while, perhaps, you will find the rest and change agreeable."

Mona thought a few moments before replying.

Her only objection to going with Mrs. Montague was she feared she might meet people whom she had known and associated with before her uncle died. She dreaded to be ignored or treated rudely by old acquaintances. She could not forget her recent experience at Macy's.

But she reasoned that she might not see any one whom she knew; she had never met Mrs. Montague in society, and her circle of friends might be entirely different from those with whom she had mingled. She longed for a respite from ceaseless stitching, and for some change of scene, and she finally resolved to go.

"Why, yes, I am perfectly willing to attend you if you wish," she said at last.

"Thank you—you have relieved my mind of quite a burden, for I feared you might decline my request," Mrs. Montague returned, and then went away to do her packing.

They were to leave New York that afternoon, but Mona had not once thought that Louis Hamblin would be likely to be one of the party, until he joined Mrs. Montague at the station.

There were a dozen or fifteen people in the party, and the young man was devotedly attentive to a pretty dark-eyed girl, who was addressed as Kitty McKenzie.

His eyes lighted with a flash of pleasure, however, the moment he caught sight of Mona, although he betrayed no other sign that he had ever seen her before.

The fair girl flushed with indignation at this slight.

Not because she was at all anxious to have him take notice of her, but because he failed to treat her, in the presence of his friends and social equals, with the courtesy which he had always been so eager to show her elsewhere.

It was a very gay party, and, as a drawing-room car had been chartered for their especial use, there was nothing to impose any restraint upon them, and mirth and pleasure reigned.

Two-thirds of the company were young people, and Kitty McKenzie was one of the merriest of the group, and apparently a great favorite, while it could be readily seen that the attentions of Louis Hamblin were very acceptable to her—her every look and smile, when conversing with him, indicating that he was far more to her than an ordinary acquaintance.

When they arrived at their destination carriages were found to be in waiting to take the party to Hazeldean, the residence of Mr. Wellington, who was to entertain the company for the ensuing week.

A drive of a mile brought them to the fine estate, where an

imposing mansion stood in the middle of a beautiful park. The interior of the dwelling was in perfect keeping with its exterior—luxury and beauty prevailed on every hand, and it was really an ideal place in which to entertain a numerous company.

The wide, mammoth hall ran the whole length of the house, while numerous rooms opened into it, with wide doors sliding upward, so that almost the whole of the lower floor could be made into one grand room. The floors were of hard wood, and polished to the last degree of brightness, and were, as Kitty McKenzie merrily remarked, while she executed a gay pirouette on entering. "just capital for dancing."

The upper stories were equally spacious, and luxuriously furnished—it really seemed like a great hotel, only far more home-like and comfortable.

The guests were soon assigned to their apartments, and Mona was gratified to find that, instead of being consigned to some remote corner of the great house, she had a cozy room opening directly into the one occupied by Mrs. Montague.

CHAPTER XV

A GAY COMPANY AT HAZELDEAN

The week that followed was one never to be forgotten. Such feasting and merry-making, such excursions, and card parties, and dancing parties Mona had never witnessed.

She had read of such scenes occurring in the great manor-houses of England, and had often thought that she should like to witness something of the kind; but she did not imagine that Americans had yet attained the art of displaying such magnificent hospitality. It was a carnival, indeed, from the evening of their arrival until the morning of their departure.

It was the month of February, there was no snow on the ground, and the weather was very mild and more like early spring, than winter, so that every morning there was planned an excursion of some kind—either a drive or a canter on horseback to different points of interest in that picturesque section, which everybody appeared to enjoy as well as if all nature had been at the height of its glory in midsummer.

Mona, of course, was never invited to join these excursions; she was regarded as nothing but a seamstress or a maid, and most of the company would have scorned the idea of thus associating with her upon equal terms.

Her heart often swelled with bitter pain as she watched a gay cavalcade ride away through the park, for she dearly loved horseback riding, and she well knew that six months previous she would have been most cordially welcomed by every member of that merry company.

She wondered what had become of her pretty saddle-horse, Jet, and her uncles proud steed, Banquo, and sighed regretfully as she reviewed the happy past, when they four— for the horses had seemed almost human—had roamed over the country together. She sometimes even longed to be back in New York among her piles of sewing, for she had not enough to do now to occupy her time, and it often hung heavily on her hands, thus allowing painful memories to depress her.

The third morning after their arrival, just as a gay party was on the point of starting off, Mona, being at liberty, thought she would slip down to the library and try to find an entertaining book to pass away the long hours before lunch.

She was half-way down stairs, when Kitty McKenzie came running breathlessly back, looking flushed and exceedingly disappointed over something.

"Oh, dear!" she cried, as she was passing Mona; "I tripped in my riding-habit, and have ripped the facing so badly that I must change it and go in the carriage with mamma. It is too bad, for I had the loveliest pony to ride."

"Have you ripped it too badly to have it repaired?" Mona asked, sorry to have the gay girl deprived of her coveted pleasure.

"Yes, for it takes me forever to mend anything. I am a wretched bungler with my needle," she confessed, with engaging frankness, but with a conscious blush.

"Let me see it," and Mona stooped to examine the rip. "This is not so bad, after all," she continued, cheerfully. "Just come to my room, and I will catch it up for you; I can do it in less time than it would take to change your dress."

"*Can* you? Oh, that will be so good of you!" and, delighted that she was not to be deprived of her ride, Miss Kitty followed Mona, with a bright face and an eager step.

Five minutes sufficed for our young seamstress to make the garment wearable, and then she told Miss McKenzie that if she would bring the habit to her upon her return, she would repair it more thoroughly.

The kind-hearted girl was very grateful.

"How kind you are to do it!" she cried, as Mona smoothed the heavy folds into place, then, with a sudden impulse and a sympathetic look into the fair face of the seamstress, she added: "What a pity it is that you have to stay here all by yourself, while the rest of us are having such delightful times! Why cannot you come with us, Miss Richards? I will make mamma let you go with her—there is an extra seat in that carriage."

"Thank you; you are very good to suggest it, Miss McKenzie, but I cannot go," Mona answered, with a flush, but touched that the girl should wish her to share her pleasures.

"I am sure you would enjoy it, for you are young, and it is too bad to be obliged to stay indoors this delightful weather,

Mrs. Georgie Sheldon

and I imagine, if the truth were known, you could be as gay as anybody, while truly," with an arch, winsome glance. "I believe you are the prettiest girl here. Do you know how to dance?"

"Yes."

"Then I think I can manage it—if you would like it, Miss Richards—to have you join the german this evening; will you?"

"You are very thoughtful, Miss McKenzie," Mona replied, appreciatively, "but I should feel out of place, even if others were as kindly disposed as yourself."

"You have had trouble—you have lost friends," Miss Kitty remarked, glancing at her black dress.

"Yes—all that I had in the world," Mona returned, with a quivering lip and a sigh that was almost a sob; for the sweet girl's kindly interest moved her deeply.

"I am sorry," said her companion, simply, but sincerely. Then she continued, with heartiness: "But let me count myself your friend after this—will you? I think you are very nice, and I believe it would be very easy to love you—you poor, lonely child!" and before Mona realized her intention, she had stooped and kissed her softly on the cheek.

She did not give her any opportunity to reply, but tripped away, flushing over her own impulsive familiarity.

She looked back over her shoulder as she reached the door and added:

"Good-by, Miss Richards; remember, you and I are to be

friends; and thank you ever so much for mending my dress."

She was gone before Mona could answer, even to tell her that she was very welcome, but her heart warmed toward the bright, genial maiden, and she stood listening, with a smile on her lips, to the sound of her little feet pattering down the stairs, and the next moment she caught her merry laugh as some one swung her lightly into her saddle.

Then Mona went down to the library, where she selected a book, and then, finding the room empty, she decided to remain where she was for a while.

Rolling a great easy-chair into a deep bay-window, she nestled, with a feeling of pleasure, in its cozy depths, and was soon deeply absorbed in the contents of her book.

She must have been reading half an hour when a slight sound in another portion of the room startled her. Turning to see what had caused it, she saw Louis Hamblin standing between the parted portieres of an archway, and gazing upon her, a smile of triumph on his handsome face.

Mona sprang from her chair, looking the surprise she felt, for she did not suppose he was in the house.

"Do not rise, Miss Richards," said the young man, as he came forward. "It is really a great pleasure to find you here, but I pray that you will not allow me to disturb you."

"I thought you had gone with the party," the young girl said, hardly knowing how to reply to him, but deeply annoyed by his presence.

"No; I had a raging toothache all night, so had to make up my rest this morning and have but just eaten breakfast. But sit down, Miss Richards; everybody has gone off and left me behind; I am lonely, and nothing would suit me better than a social little chat with yourself," he concluded, with obnoxious familiarity.

Mona drew her graceful form to its full height, while her red lips curled scornfully.

"Thank you, but it might be considered in bad taste for one in Mr. Hamblin's position to be found chatting socially with his aunt's seamstress, whom he is not supposed to know," she said, a note of sarcasm in her tone.

The young man laughed out lightly.

"Ah! you resent it because I did not recognize you the day we came to Hazeldean," he returned; "but you will forgive me, I know, when I tell you that I avoided betraying the fact of our previous acquaintance simply for your own good. I feared it might make you conspicuous if I saluted you, as I wished to do, and my aunt is very particular about the proprieties of life."

Mona smiled proudly. She failed to perceive how a courteous recognition could have made her conspicuous or violated in any way the most rigid laws of etiquette.

"In that case we will continue to observe the proprieties of life upon all occasions," she dryly remarked.

He read her thoughts, and was keenly stung by her words.

"Forgive me," he said, with an assumption of regret and humility, thinking thus the better to gain his end; "had I realized that you would have been so wounded I should have acted very differently. I assure you I will never offend you in the same way again."

"Pray do not be troubled," Mona coldly retorted. "I had no thought of resenting anything which you might consider proper to do. If I thought of the matter at all, it was only in connection with the generally accepted principles of courtesy and good-breeding."

Mr. Hamblin flushed hotly at this keen shaft, but he ignored it, and changed the subject.

"I am sorry to have interrupted you in your reading, Miss Richards. What have you that is interesting?"

"Victor Hugo's 'Les Miserables,'" Mona briefly replied.

"Have you?" the young man eagerly demanded, "I was searching for that book only yesterday. May I look at it one moment? McArthur and I had quite a discussion upon a point regarding Father Madelaine, and we were unable to settle it because we could not find the book."

Mona quietly passed the volume to him; but a blank look overspread his face as he took it.

"Why, it is the original!" he exclaimed, "and I do not read French readily. Are you familiar with it?"

"Oh, yes," and Mona smiled slightly.

She had been accounted the finest French scholar in her class.

Mr. Hamblin regarded her wonderingly.

"Where did you learn French to be able to read it at sight?"

Mrs. Georgie Sheldon

he inquired.

"At school."

"But—I thought—" he began, and stopped confused.

"You thought that a common seamstress must necessarily be ignorant, as well as poor," Mona supplemented: "that she would not be likely to have opportunities or ambition for self-improvement. Well, Mr. Hamblin, perhaps some girls in such a position would not, but I honestly believe that there is many a poor girl, who has had to make her own way in life, who is better educated than many of the so-called society belles of to-day."

"I believe it, too, if you are a specimen," her companion returned, as he gazed admiringly into Mona's flushed and animated face.

"At any rate," he added, "you are far more beautiful than the majority of society girls."

"Mr. Hamblin will please reserve his compliments for ears more eager for and more accustomed to them," Mona retorted, with a frown of annoyance.

"Why are you so proud and scornful toward me, Miss Richards?" he appealingly asked. "Can you not see that my admiration for you is genuine—that I really desire to be your friend? And why have you avoided me so persistently of late—why have you rejected my flowers?"

"Because," Mona frankly answered, and meeting his glance squarely, "I know, and *you* know, that it is not proper for you to offer, nor for me to accept, such attentions, even if I desired them."

"I am my own master; you are your own mistress, if, as you say, you are alone in the world; consequently, such a matter lies between ourselves, without regard to what others might consider as 'proper,' And I may as well make an open confession first as last," he went on, eagerly, and bending nearer to her, with a flushed face. "Ruth, my beautiful Ruth, I love you—I began to love you that morning when we met on the steps before our own door, and every day has only increased my affection for you."

A startled look swept over Mona's face, which had now grown very pale. She had not had a suspicion that she was destined to hear such a declaration as this; it had taken her wholly unawares, and for a moment she was speechless.

But she soon recovered herself.

"Stop!" she haughtily cried "you have no right to use such language to me; you would not presume—you would not *dare* to do so upon so brief an acquaintance, if I stood upon an equal footing with you, socially. It is only because I am poor and unprotected—because you simply wish to amuse yourself for a time. You would not dare to repeat in the presence of Mrs. Montague what you have just said to me. Now let me pass, if you please, and never presume to address me again as you have to-day."

The indignant girl looked like some beautiful princess as she stood before him and thus resented the insult he had offered her.

Her slight form was held proudly erect, her small head was uplifted with an air of scorn, her eyes blazed forth angry contempt as they met his, while her whole bearing indicated a conscious superiority which both humiliated and stung her would-be suitor.

Mrs. Georgie Sheldon

She had never appeared so beautiful to him before. Her face was as pure as a pearl; her glossy hair, falling loosely away from her white forehead, was simply coiled at the back of her small head, thus revealing its symmetrical proportions to the best advantages. Her great brown eyes glowed and scintillated, her nostrils dilated, her lips quivered with outraged pride and delicacy.

Her dress of dead black fell in soft, clinging folds about her slender form, making her seem taller than she really was, while one hand had been raised to enforce the commands which she had laid upon him.

He thought her the fairest vision he had ever seen, in spite of her indignation against him, and if she had sought to fascinate him—to weave the spell of her witchery more effectually about him, she could have taken no surer way to do so.

He could not fail to admire her spirit—it but served to glorify her in his sight, and made him more eager than before to conquer her.

"Nay, do not leave me thus—do not be so bitter against me, my peerless Ruth," he pleaded. "Perhaps I have been premature in my avowal, but I beg that you will not despise me on that account. Do not judge me so harshly. Lay my impatience rather to my eagerness to win you. I would do anything in the world to make you love me, and now, I fear, I have only been driving you farther from me. I love you, honestly and sincerely, my beautiful Ruth, and I would not only dare to confess it to my aunt, but proclaim it before the world, if that would serve to prove it to you. Ah! teach me how to woo you, my darling; give me but a crumb of hope upon which to feed, and I will try to be satisfied until you can learn to have more confidence in me."

He reached forth his arms as if he would have infolded her; and Mona, who for the moment had been rendered spell-bound by the swift rush of burning words that he had poured forth, seemed suddenly electrified by the act.

She felt both insulted and humiliated by this premature avowal of a love that had not received the slightest encouragement from her, and she recoiled from him with a gesture of contempt.

"I wonder how you have dared to say this to me," she cried, in a voice that quivered with indignation, "when in my very presence you have shown another attentions such as a man has a right to bestow only upon the woman whom he intends to marry. But for the respect I owe myself and my sex, I would like to brand you with a mark that would betray your disloyalty to the world, and make Miss McKenzie despise you as I do; being only a weak woman, however, I must content myself with simply manifesting my scorn, and by telling you to go!" and she pointed authoritatively toward the door with one white taper finger.

A hot, crimson flush dyed the young man's white face with a sense of shame, such as he had never before experienced in the presence of any one, while the purple veins stood out in ridges upon his forehead.

He was completely cowed before her. Conscious himself of the insincerity and unworthiness of his declaration, he knew that she also had read him like an open book, and the knowledge made him fearfully angry; while to be foiled in his purpose and browbeaten by this girl, whom he imagined to be only what she seemed, was more than his indomitable spirit could tamely submit to.

"A love like mine is not to be despised, and you shall yet

find it so," he muttered between his tightly shut teeth.

Mona would not deign him a reply, but standing in the same attitude, she again motioned him to go.

Unable longer to endure the unflinching gaze of her clear, scornful eyes, he shrank back through the portieres, which instantly fell into place again, and Mona, with a smile of disdain curving her red lips, went back to her seat by the window.

But all enjoyment in her book was gone; she was much excited, for she had been greatly shaken by the interview and made to feel her position as she never yet had done; and after sitting a few moments gazing sadly out of the window she again went up to her own room.

CHAPTER XVI

MONA LEARNS SOMETHING OF RAY

That same evening as Mona was passing up stairs from the laundry, whither she had been to press out the ruffles of a dress, which Mrs. Montague wished to wear at the german a few hours later, she heard the hall-bell ring a resounding peal.

She hastened on, for she did not wish to be observed by strangers, but as she reached the upper landing, she caught some hearty words of welcome from Mr. Wellington, the host, and knew that another guest had arrived.

But she suddenly stopped short, and the color receded from her cheeks, while her heart beat with quick, heavy throbs as she heard the name of Palmer pronounced.

"Can it be possible that Ray Palmer is the newcomer?" she asked herself.

She leaned over the banister, curiosity and an eager longing prompting her to ascertain if he were the guest.

But no, it was not Ray.

She saw instead an elderly gentleman, of benevolent and

genial appearance, who seemed to be a valued friend of the family, judging from the enthusiastic greeting which his host accorded him.

"Well, well, Palmer, you are rather late in the week, but none the less welcome on that account," remarked Mr. Wellington. "We have been having gay times, and I have only needed your presence to make my enjoyment complete. But where is that precious son of yours? How is it that Raymond did not come with you?"

Mona held her breath at this.

The question had told her that the new arrival was Ray's father, and that the young man had also been invited to join the gay company that was sojourning beneath the hospitable roof.

She leaned farther over the railing that she might not fail to catch Mr. Palmer's reply.

"Oh," answered that gentleman, as he removed his overcoat and gloves, "Ray is not yet quite as strong as we could wish, although he calls himself well, and he feels hardly equal to much dissipation as yet. Besides, he is rather depressed just now."

"Over the affair of the diamonds, I suppose?" Mr. Wellington observed.

"Yes, and—some other matter that troubles him."

"I am very sorry. I was depending upon him to help amuse some of our fair young guests," said his host. Then he added, with considerable interest: "Any new developments regarding that remarkable robbery?"

"No; and I do not imagine there ever will be," Mr. Palmer gravely returned.

"Then you have given up all hope of ever recovering them?"

"Well, almost, though I have a detective on the lookout yet, and he thinks if he can get track of the thief in this case, she will prove to be the very woman that he has been searching for during the last three years. He imagines that she is the same one who was concerned in a bold swindle in Chicago about that time."

"Well, I sincerely hope that he will be successful in finding her; such wickedness should not be allowed to prosper," said Mr. Wellington. "I am really sorry about Ray, though—he is such capital company, and there are six or eight wonderfully pretty girls here who will be deeply disappointed when they learn that he is not coming at all."

The two gentlemen passed into the drawing-room just then, and Mona heard nothing more.

She deeply sighed, and continued to stand there for some moments lost in thought.

She could not really make up her mind whether she was more disappointed than rejoiced over Ray's failure to meet this engagement.

It would have been very pleasant to see him again, but it would also have been very humiliating to have him find her there in the capacity of a servant, and ignore her on this account, as Louis Hamblin had done. She still felt most keenly his apparent neglect of her during her troubles, and of course, being entirely ignorant of what had occurred, she attributed it to the most unworthy motives, which, however, did not help to reconcile her to the loss of his friendship.

She gathered from what Mr. Palmer had said about his not being quite strong yet that Ray had been ill, and she wondered, too, what he had meant by his being depressed on account of some other matter that was troubling him.

She had also learned something new about the robbery, of which she had only had a faint hint from the little item which she had read in the paper on the day she went to Mrs. Montague's. She gleaned now that Ray had in some way been responsible for the loss—or, at least felt himself to be so to some extent.

She wished that she could have heard more about him, and she was conscious of a deeper sense of loneliness and friendliness, from this little rift in the cloud that had shut her out of the world where once she had been so happy.

Another sigh escaped her as she slowly turned to go on to her room and almost unconsciously she cried out, with a little sob of pain and longing:

"Oh, Ray, Ray!"

"Aha!"

The ejaculation startled the young girl beyond measure. She did not dream that there was any one near her. She had been so absorbed in observing Mr. Palmer and listening to what had occurred in the lower hall, and in her own sad thoughts, that she was unconscious that any one had stolen up on her unawares, and had also been a witness to the interview between Mr. Palmer and Mr. Wellington, until this exclamation made her look up. She found herself again face to face with Louis Hamblin.

"Aha!" he repeated, in a tone of triumph, but with a frown upon his brow; "that explains why my suit was so disdained this morning! So you know and—love Mr. Raymond Palmer! My pretty Ruth, pray tell me how this young Apollo managed to inspire the princess of sewing-girls with such tender sentiments, that I may profit by his successful method."

"Let me pass!" Mona commanded, as, straight as a young palm, she confronted the insolent fellow with blazing cheeks and flashing eyes.

"It makes you wonderfully pretty to get angry," he returned, with a gleeful chuckle; "but I am not going to let you pass until you tell me when and where you made young Palmer's acquaintance," and he continued to stand directly in her path.

"Do you imagine that you can *compel* me to say *anything*?" Mona burst forth, with stinging contempt, her patience all gone. "Let this be the last time that you ever waylay or persecute me with your attentions, for, I give you fair warning, a repetition of such conduct on your part will send me straight to Mrs. Montague with a full report of it."

The young man looked decidedly crestfallen at this spirited threat.

There was but one person in the world of whom he stood in awe, and that was his aunt, Margaret Montague.

He well knew that it would not be for his interest to offend her, and, of all things, he would dread most a revelation of what had occurred in the library that morning, notwithstanding he had affirmed to Mona that he was willing to proclaim his affection before her and the whole world.

Mrs. Georgie Sheldon

Besides, if it should come to the ears of Kitty McKenzie, his prospects of a marriage with that pretty and wealthy young lady would be blighted, and no end of trouble would follow, for Mrs. Montague had determined to effect a union between them, and if he should go contrary to her wishes, she could make it very uncomfortable for him pecuniarily.

Still, he was deeply smitten with the beautiful young seamstress, and was rapidly becoming more so every time he met her.

He had promised himself the pleasure of a secret flirtation with her, while at the same time he intended to continue his attentions to Miss McKenzie in public, and he did not like to be balked in his purpose.

He saw that he could never intimidate her into any concessions; she was far too high-spirited and straightforward; so he must adopt other measures if he would win.

"Certainly you shall pass, if you wish," he said, respectfully, as he stepped aside; "but please do not be quite so unkind; and, by the way, can you tell me what the old codger down below meant by his son being upset about the diamonds?"

He knew well enough, for of course he had seen the accounts of the affair in the papers; but he had an object in wishing to find out how much Mona knew.

"No, I cannot," she coldly replied, as, with uplifted head and haughty bearing, she passed him and entered Mrs. Montague's room.

While this incident was occurring in the hall of the second story, Mr. Amos Palmer was being introduced to the company below.

His advent caused quite a flutter of excitement among the young ladies; for most of them were acquainted with Ray, who for nearly two years had been a great favorite in society, and they had been led to expect that he was to join their company at Hazeldean.

Great disappointment was expressed when they learned that he was not likely to put in an appearance at all, and Mr. Palmer began to feel sorry that he had not insisted upon having his son come with him.

Mr. Wellington was full of wit and pleasantry, and made merry, as he went around the room with his friend, to introduce the strangers to him.

As they came to Mrs. Montague, he was somewhat surprised when the lady greeted Mr. Palmer with great cordiality.

"I have already the pleasure of Mr. Palmer's acquaintance," she said, with one of her most alluring smiles, as she extended her hand to him, and forthwith she entered into conversation with him, thus effectually chaining him to her side.

He seemed only too well pleased to linger there—he was, in fact, a willing captive to her wiles, a circumstance which the bright eyes of the younger portion of the company did not fail to observe and to comment upon, with something of amusement, and not a little of the match-making spirit of their own mammas.

"Girls!" exclaimed Alice Farwell, a gay, dashing beauty of twenty, to a group of friends whom she had coaxed into a corner, "do you know that a romance has begun here this evening?—a romance that will not be long in culminating in matrimony? Oh! don't go to pluming your feathers," she continued, as there was a general flutter, "for we *young* Americans will not figure in the story at all, though we may possibly be invited to the wedding. Oh, if it should prove to be the only match of the season!" and with a long-drawn sigh, she glanced mischievously across the room, toward the recent arrival, who was apparently oblivious of all, save the attractions of the charming Mrs. Montague.

Talk of match-making mammas!

This bevy of young girls became so engrossed in watching the progress of the romance which was then being enacted in their presence, that they forgot to flirt themselves, and took pains to help it on in every possible way.

"It will be just the nicest match in the world," said Edith Brown, delightfully. "Mr. Palmer is a fine-looking old gentleman, and Mrs. Montague, though she seems a great deal younger, will make him a lovely wife."

"It will be so suitable, too, for they are both rich, and stand high in society," whispered a third, with an eye to worldly prosperity.

"And she can have all the diamonds she wants," chimed in a little miss of sixteen, "for he is a diamond merchant, you know."

This remark caused a general laugh, and then the conversation turned upon the recent robbery, which was discussed at some length.

"Who would have thought of decoying Ray Palmer into Doctor Wesselhoff's retreat?" exclaimed Alice Farwell. "It was a very daring thing to do. By the way, I wonder what the reason *is* young Palmer did not come with his father? I can't quite believe he isn't well enough, for I saw him only the day before we left New York, and he was walking down Broadway with as much energy as any one, only he looked a trifle pale and anxious."

"I wish he would come up for the grand hop on next Monday," said Edith Brown. "He is capital company, and a delightful partner. I am going to coax Mr. Palmer to send for him. Come, girls, he has monopolized our pretty widow long enough; suppose we break up the conference and put in our petition."

The merry maidens were nothing loath to have another handsome escort added to their number, and, headed by the audacious Edith, they went in a body to make their request of Mr. Palmer.

"Well, it is too bad to have Ray miss all this," he said, smilingly, when they allowed him an opportunity to reply. "I believe it would do him good to come, and he could not help enjoying himself here," he added, as his genial eyes rested on the bright faces before him. "I believe I will telegraph him in the morning."

The fair petitioners were satisfied with their success, and, dinner being announced just then, the subject was dropped for the time.

After dinner there was a progressive whist party for an hour, at the end of which there was considerable fun occasioned by the awarding of the prizes, and after that everybody was ready for the german.

But great disappointment was expressed when they found that there was one lady lacking to enable them all to participate in the dance.

"What shall we do?—no one wants to sit and look on—it is very stupid, and the rest of us wouldn't enjoy it, either, to have any wallflowers about," Kitty McKenzie regretfully remarked. "Oh! Mrs. Montague," she added, as if the idea had just occurred to her, "there is your pretty seamstress; may she not come, just for this once?"

Mrs. Montague hesitated.

"Please," persisted the generous-hearted Kitty; "she is very nice and lady-like; I am sure no one could object to her, and I know she would enjoy it."

Two or three others seconded the proposal, and the lady then gave her consent, though with evident reluctance.

Miss Kitty, all elated with the success of her project, and never dreaming that Mona would not enjoy it, ran away to bring her down.

She found her in her own room reading a recent magazine.

"Come," she said, with gleaming eyes, "you are to join us in the german. I have Mrs. Montague's permission, and we are all waiting for you."

"I thank you very much Miss McKenzie," Mona responded, flushing, "but I do not believe I will go down."

"Oh, do; we need just one more lady, and some of the gentlemen will have to sit it out if you do not. Miss Nellie Wellington has to play for us, or she would dance, so please come," Miss Kitty urged, looking disappointed enough over Mona's unexpected refusal.

Mona shrank from joining the dancers, or from mingling

with the company, for several reasons.

She had no heart for dancing, so soon after her uncle's death; she disliked to go among people who would regard her as an inferior, and only tolerate her presence because she would help to "fill out," while last, but not least, she wished to keep out of Louis Hamblin's way.

But she did not like to appear disobliging or unappreciative of Miss McKenzie's kindness, and a bright idea suddenly occurred to her.

"I really do not care to dance, Miss McKenzie, although it is very thoughtful of you to invite me; but if it will be agreeable to the company, I will take Miss Wellington's place at the piano, and she can make up the desired number."

"Oh, *can* you play?" cried Kitty, both astonished and delighted. "That will help us out, and I am sure it is very nice of you to offer, for I think it is awfully stupid to play for dancing. Come, then, and I know everybody will be surprised as well as pleased."

And winding her arm about the slender waist of the fair seamstress, they went down stairs together, Miss McKenzie chatting away as sociably as if they had always been friends and equals.

Mrs. Montague lifted her eyebrows with well-bred astonishment when the young lady informed the company that Miss Richards preferred to preside at the piano, and a number of others appealed to share her surprise, and looked somewhat skeptical, also.

They were more amazed still when she modestly took her seat and began her duties, for Mona was perfectly at home in music, and soon made the room ring with inspiring melody for the eager dancers.

"Who is that beautiful and talented girl?" Amos Palmer asked of his host, when the young people were tired of dancing, and Mona quietly withdrew from the room.

"Her name is Ruth Richards, I believe," Mr. Wellington replied.

"You 'believe!' Isn't she a guest here?" inquired Mr. Palmer, with surprise.

"No; she is simply a maid in the employ of Mrs. Montague."

"Well, it is a great pity."

"What is a great pity?"

"That such a lovely young lady should have to serve any one in that capacity; she is beautiful and talented enough to fill any position."

And this was Amos Palmer's opinion regarding Ray's unknown lady-love.

CHAPTER XVII

MRS. MONTAGUE QUESTIONS MONA

"Where did you learn to play the piano, Ruth?" Mrs. Montague inquired the next morning, while Mona was engaged in assisting her to dress, and she turned a searching glance upon her as she put the question.

To conceal the flush that mounted to her brow, Mona stooped to pick up a pin.

It had not occurred to her, when she offered to play for the dancing the previous evening, that such proficiency in music would be regarded as something very unusual in a sewing-girl, and might occasion remark.

Her only object had been to oblige Kitty McKenzie and avoid dancing with the guests.

"I had a relative who gave me lessons for a while," she said, in reply to Mrs. Montague's query.

"For a while!" repeated that lady, who had not been unobservant of the flush. "You finger the piano as if you had been accustomed to diligent practice all your life, and you must have had the best of instruction, too."

Mrs. Georgie Sheldon

"I am very fond of music, and it was never any task to me to practice," Mona remarked. Then she added, to change the topic: "Shall I baste this ruffle in the full width, or shall I set it down a trifle?"

Mrs. Montague smiled at the tact of her pretty companion, in thus attempting to draw her attention to her own affairs.

A good many things had convinced her of late that her seamstress had not been reared in poverty, and certain suspicions, that had startled her when she first saw her, were beginning to force themselves again upon her.

"You can set it down a trifle," she replied; then she asked, persistently returning to the previous question: "Why do you not give music lessons, since you play so well, instead of sewing for your living? I should suppose it would be a much more congenial occupation."

"There are so many music teachers, and one needs a reputation in order to obtain pupils; besides, people would doubtless regard me as too young to have had much experience in teaching. There, I have finished this—is there anything else I can do for you?" and Mona laid the dress she had been at work upon on a chair, and stood awaiting further orders.

"Yes; the buckle on this slipper needs to be more securely fastened. It is true that there are legions of music teachers. Was this relative of yours a teacher?"

"Oh, no; he simply bore the expense of my instruction."

"I suppose he cannot be living, or you would not be sewing for me," Mrs. Montague remarked, with another searching glance.

"No," was the brief reply, and hot tears rushed to Mona's eyes, blinding her so that she could hardly see where to put her needle.

She then made some remark to the effect that she needed some stronger silk, and left the room to hide the grief which she found so hard to control.

"Aha! this relative must be the friend for whom she is in mourning—he cannot have been dead very long, for the girl is unable to speak of him without tears," muttered Mrs. Montague, thoughtfully, a heavy frown settling on her brow. "There is some mystery about her which I am bound to ferret out; she is exceedingly reticent about herself—I wonder if my suspicions can be correct?" she continued, her face settling into hard, revengeful lines. "She certainly looks enough like that girl to be her child. If I were sure, I would not spare her; I would crush her, for the hate that I bore her mother, notwithstanding she is so useful to me. Ha, ha!" and the laugh was exceedingly bitter, "it would seem like the irony of fate to have her child thrown thus into my power. But if she is Mona Montague why does she call herself Ruth Richards? what can be her object? Can it be possible," she added, with a startled look, "that she has been told her history, and she has engaged herself to me with the purpose of trying to obtain the proofs of it? Is she deep enough for that? or has she been advised to adopt such a course? She seems to be very frank and innocent, intent only upon doing her work well and pleasing me. Yet, if she should get hold of any of those proofs, she could make a great deal of trouble for me. I believe I shall have to destroy them, although I always feel as if a ghost were haunting me whenever I touch them. I shall never be satisfied until I learn Ruth's history. I'll attack her about the Palmers; if she is Mona Montague—the girl that Ray Palmer loves—she certainly will betray herself if I take her unawares; although she did not appear to know

Mrs. Georgie Sheldon

Mr. Palmer, last evening."

Mona returned at this moment, and Mrs. Montague's musings were cut short.

The young girl had recovered her self-control, and was as calm and collected as usual; even more so, for she had told herself that she must be more on her guard or she would betray her identity.

Mrs. Montague appeared to have forgotten all about their recent conversation, and chatted sociably about various topics for a while. But suddenly she asked:

"Did you observe the new arrival last night, Ruth?"

"Do you mean that portly gentleman, who is slightly bald, and with whom you went out for refreshments?" Mona inquired, lifting a frank, inquiring look to her companion, though her heart beat fast at this reference to Ray's father.

"Yes; he is very fine-looking, don't you think so?"

"Perhaps so—rather," replied Mona, reflectively.

"That is 'rather' doubtful praise, I am afraid," observed Mrs. Montague, with a light laugh. "I think he is a very handsome old gentleman, and he is certainly a decidedly entertaining companion. You know who he is, I suppose."

"I do not think that I heard anybody address him by name while I was in the drawing-room; of course; I was not introduced to any one," Mona evasively answered.

"His name is Palmer," Mrs. Montague remarked, as she bent a searching look upon the young girl.

But Mona had herself well in hand now, and she made no sign that the name was a familiar one to her.

"He has a son who is strikingly good looking, too," Mrs. Montague continued. "I met them both at a reception in New York a little while ago, and was greatly attracted to them, though just now the young man is rather unhappy—in fact, he is wearing the willow for some girl whom he imagines he loves."

Mrs. Montague paused to note the effect of this conversation, but Mona had finished fastening the buckle on the slipper, and quietly taken up some other work, though her pulses were beating like trip-hammers.

"It seems," the woman resumed, her keen eyes never leaving the fair face opposite to her, "that he has long been very fond of a girl whose surname is the same as mine—a Miss Mona Montague. She was a niece of that wealthy Mr. Dinsmore, who died so suddenly in New York a short time ago."

It seemed to Mona that her heart must leap from her bosom as she listened to this reference to herself; but, with every appearance of perfect composure, she measured off some ribbon that she was making into bows, and severed it with a sharp clip of her scissors.

"Perhaps you do not know whom I mean," said Mrs. Montague, and paused, determined to make the girl speak.

"Oh, yes, I have heard of him, and I remember reading the notice of his death in a paper," Mona compelled herself to say, without betraying anything of the pain which smote her heart in recurring thus to her great loss.

Mrs. Montague frowned.

She was not progressing as well as she could have wished in her "pumping" operation; but she meant to probe the matter as far as she dared.

"Well," she went on, "this niece was supposed by everybody to be Mr. Dinsmore's heiress; but a discarded wife suddenly made her appearance, after his death, and claimed the whole of his property, and the girl was left without a penny. She must have been terribly cut up about it, for she suddenly disappeared, and cannot be found, and it is this that has so upset young Palmer. He had not committed himself, his father informed me, but was just on the point of declaring his love when Mr. Dinsmore died; and the girl, evidently crushed by her loss, has hidden herself so securely that no one can find her."

It was fortunate for Mona that her recent troubles had taught her something of self-control, or she must have betrayed herself at this point.

She realized that Mrs. Montague must have a purpose in relating all this to her, and feared it was to verify some suspicion regarding herself.

She now believed that the woman must know all her mother's history, and certain facts regarding her own birth, which she felt that Mr. Dinsmore had, for some reason, withheld from her. This conviction had grown upon her ever since she had been a member of her family, and she hoped, by some means, if she remained long enough with her, to learn the truth. Still she feared that if Mrs. Montague should discover that she was her husband's daughter she might be so prejudiced against her she would at once dismiss her from her employ, and she would then lose her only chance to solve the questions that puzzled her. But she found it very hard to conceal the great and sudden joy that went thrilling through her as she listened to these facts regarding Ray Palmer's affection for and his loyalty to her.

He had not been unworthy and faithless, as she had imagined; there had been some good reason why he had not come to her during the early days of her trouble. He might have been called suddenly away from New York on business and not been able to return until her home was broken up; and now he was grieving—"wearing the willow," as Mrs. Montague expressed it—because he could not find her. He loved her! he had been upon the point of telling her so, and this blissful knowledge made the world seem suddenly bright again to the hitherto depressed and grieving girl.

But it would never do to betray anything of this, for then Mrs. Montague would know at once that *she* was Mona Montague; so she made no sign that she was any more interested in this little romance regarding Ray Palmer's love, than she would have been in that of any stranger. She even forced herself to ignore him altogether, and ask, in a matter-of-fact way:

"Is it not strange, if Mr. Dinsmore had a wife living, that he did not make some provision for his niece, by will?"

"The girl *isn't* Mona Montague after all, or she never would have asked such a question with that innocent air," said Mrs. Montague to herself, with some disappointment; "the strange resemblance must be only a coincidence, striking though it is. But I would really like to know where Walter Dinsmore's niece is. I feel as if I had an enemy in ambush all the time, for she would have it in her power to do me a great deal of harm if she could prove her identity. I am half sorry that Ruth doesn't prove to be she, for having her here, under my eye, I could manage her capitally."

Mrs. Georgie Sheldon

"Why, the papers discussed all that at the time," she remarked aloud, with some surprise. "There was considerable excitement over the affair, and sympathy was very strong for the niece. Didn't you read about it?"

"No, I was very much engaged just then, and I did not read any account of it. There, these bows are ready, and I will sew them to the dress," Mona concluded, rising to get the garment, but trembling with nervous excitement in every limb.

"Ah!" she added, glancing at her fingers, three of which were stained with blood. "I have pricked myself with my needle; I hope I have not soiled the ribbon. No, fortunately, I have not," as she carefully examined it, "but I will step into the bath-room to wash my hands. I will not be long," and she immediately left the room again. She had purposely run the needle into her delicate flesh to obtain this respite, for she felt as if she could no longer endure the trying conversation.

"Oh, how she has tortured me!" she sobbed, as she swung the door to after her, and dashed from her eyes the tears which she could no longer restrain. "I could not bear it another moment, and I must not give way, even now, or she will see that I am unnerved, but I cannot be wholly wretched now that I know that *Ray loves me*!"

A vivid blush mounted to her brow as she whispered the sweet words, and she dashed the cold water over her burning cheeks to cool them.

"Ah!" she continued; "I judged him wrongfully, and I am sorry. It will be all right if we can but meet again. It must be true that he loved me, he must have confessed it, or his father would not have told Mrs. Montague so."

She hastily dried her face, and hands, then composing herself, returned to Mrs. Montague's room to find her with her dress on and looking very fair and lovely in the delicately tinted blue cashmere, with the soft ruching in the neck and sleeves and the shining satin bows at her waist.

The woman glanced sharply at Mona as she entered, but, for all that she could see, the sweet face was as serene as if she were intent only upon her duties as waiting-maid, instead of thrilling with joy over the knowledge of being beloved by one whom, until that hour, she had believed lost to her.

"I will submit her to one more test, and if she can stand it I shall be satisfied," she said to herself, as she fastened a beautiful pin at her throat, and then turned smilingly to Mona, but with the most innocent air in the world.

"Am I all right, Ruth? Is the dress becoming?" she asked.

"Exceedingly," Mona returned; "the color is just suited to you."

"Thank you, I wonder if Mr. Palmer will also think so. Do you know," with a conscious laugh and forced blush, but with a covert glance at the girl, "I am becoming very much interested in that gentleman. I like the son, too, but chiefly for his father's sake. By the way, young Mr. Palmer is to be here for the ball on Monday evening; at least his father is going to telegraph him to come."

"Is he?" said Mona, absently, while she appeared to be engrossed with something which she had suddenly discovered about the new morning robe. But the statement that Ray was coming to Hazeldean had given her an inward start that made every nerve in her body bound as if an electric current had been applied to them. "This skirt does not seem to hang just right," she added, dropping upon her knees, as if to ascertain the cause. "Ah! it was only caught up—it is all right now."

She smoothed the folds into place and arose, while, the breakfast-bell ringing at that moment, Mrs. Montague passed from the room, very nearly if not quite satisfied that Ruth Richards was an entirely different person from Mona Montague.

Poor over-wrought Mona, however, fled into her own chamber, and locked the door the moment she was alone.

She sank into the nearest chair, buried her face in her hands, and fell to sobbing nervously.

"How can I bear it?" she murmured. "It is perfectly dreadful to have to live such a life of deception. I never would have been guilty of it if I had not been caught just as I was; but I could not give her my real name, for she would have known at once who I am; and I do so want to find out just why my father deserted my mother, and what there was between him and Uncle Walter that was so terrible. Perhaps I never shall, but I mean to stay with her for a while and try. She is a strange woman," the young girl went on, musingly. "Sometimes I think she is kind and good, then again she seems like a designing and unprincipled person. Can it be possible that she is contemplating an alliance with Mr. Palmer? She certainly received his attentions last evening with every appearance of pleasure, and he seemed to be equally delighted with her society. I wonder if Ray will like it? Somehow the thought of it is not agreeable to me, if—if—"

A vivid blush suffused Mona's cheeks as she reached this point in her soliloquy, as if she was overcome at having allowed her thoughts to run away with her to such an extent.

"So Ray is coming to Hazeldean for the ball on Monday evening," she continued, after a while. "Shall I see him? Yes, I shall try to," with an air of resolution. "If he loves me as well as I love him, why should any foolish sensitiveness prevent my allowing him to make it manifest, if he wishes? I do not believe I have any right to ruin both our lives by hiding myself from him. I will prove him in this way; but I must see him alone, so that no one will know that I am Mona Montague, instead of Ruth Richards, the sewing-girl. What if *he* should ignore me?" she added, with sudden fear and growing very white; then, with renewed confidence: "He will not; if he has been noble enough to confess his feelings to his father, he will not hide them from me. He is noble and true, and I will not doubt him."

CHAPTER XVIII

"MY DARLING, I LOVE YOU!"

Mr. Palmer, true to his promise to the fair young guests at Hazeldean, telegraphed to Ray the next morning requesting him to come up for the ball on Monday. Later in the day he received a reply from the young man stating that he would do so, although he did not mention the hour when he should arrive.

Thursday, Friday, and Saturday were gay and busy days, for the ball was to be a grand affair, and everybody was anxious to do all possible honor to the occasion and made preparations accordingly.

Mrs. Montague, however, was not so busy but that she managed to spend a good deal of her time with Mr. Palmer, who seemed to renew his youth in her presence, and was so gallant and attentive that the young people, who were exceedingly interested in watching the progress of this middle-aged romance, were kept in a constant flutter of amused excitement. Mr. Wellington and his wife were also considerably diverted by the affair.

"I'm afraid Palmer is a 'gone goose,'" the gentleman laughingly remarked to his spouse, after they had retired to their room on Saturday evening.

"It looks like it," the lady returned; "and really," she added, with some impatience, "there is something almost ridiculous to me in seeing an old man like him dancing attendance upon a gay young widow like Mrs. Montague."

"*Young!* How old do you imagine her to be?" inquired Mr. Wellington.

"She cannot be much over thirty, and she dresses in a way to make her look even younger than that," the lady responded. "At all events, she seems like a mere girl beside portly, bald-headed Mr. Palmer, and I am afraid that he will regret it if he allows himself to become entangled in her net."

"I see that you are not in favor of the match," replied Mr. Wellington, much amused over his wife's earnestness.

"No, Will; I confess I am not," she said, gravely. "I knew Amos Palmer's first wife, and she was a devoted, care-taking, conscientious woman, never sparing herself when she could add to the comfort and happiness of her family. But this woman is entirely different—she cares very little for anything but society. I admit she is very delightful company—a charming person to have in the house at such a time as this; but I doubt her ability to make Mr. Palmer happy, and I never would have believed that he could have had his head so thoroughly turned by any woman. I thought he was bound up in making money, to leave to that handsome son of his."

"Well, it appears that Cupid can make fools of the best of us," Mr. Wellington returned, with a roguish glance at his wife; "and we do not discover the fact until the noose is irrevocably knotted about our necks. By the way, speaking of

Mrs. Georgie Sheldon

accumulating money makes me remember that Palmer had a telegram to-day, telling him that the detective whom he employed on that affair of the diamonds thinks that he is on the track of the thief at last."

"Is that so?" said Mrs. Wellington, with surprise. "Do you imagine that he will ever recover the stones?"

"He may—some of the larger ones, for they had been submitted to an expert; but I doubt if he ever sees many of them again," her husband replied.

*   *   *   *   *

During these last two days Mona had been kept steadily employed in performing various duties for Mrs. Montague.

That lady's costume for the ball was to be of great elegance and beauty.

The material was a rich garnet velvet, brocaded in white and gold, with point-lace garniture.

It had not been quite finished before they left New York, and Mona found no little difficulty in setting the many last stitches, for she had had but small experience in finishing garments of any kind, and Mrs. Montague was very particular.

It was quite late in the evening when she completed her task, and, with a sigh of relief, laid the beautiful costume upon the bed, ready for Mrs. Montague's inspection when she should come up stairs for the night.

There was something of regret also mingled with her feeling that she, too, could not join the festivities on Monday evening. She had dearly loved society during the little while she had mingled with it, and the pleasurable excitement of the last few days, which kept all the young ladies in a constant flutter, made her long to be one among them.

It was about half-past two when Mrs. Montague made her appearance, looking flushed and elated, for she had just parted from Mr. Palmer, who had begged her to attend service at the village church with him the next morning. The request was so impressively expressed that she imagined her conquest was nearly complete, and she was therefore in high spirits.

She caught sight of her ball-dress immediately upon entering the room.

"How lovely it is, Ruth," she remarked, "and you have arranged the lace very tastefully upon the corsage. I believe it will be exceedingly becoming. I only wish I could see myself as others will see me on Monday night, and know just how I am going to look. Ruth," she added, suddenly, as if inspired with a bright idea, "you are about my height; suppose you put on the dress and let me get just the effect; that is, if you are not too tired and do not mind being made a show figure, here all by ourselves."

Mona smiled slightly over the woman's vanity, but she was willing to oblige, and so signified her readiness to put the dress on, and in less than ten minutes she had metamorphosed herself from the quiet, retiring sewing-girl into a brilliant society belle.

The dress was a trifle loose for her, yet it was not a bad fit, while her pure neck and arms were as white as the costly lace, which fell in soft folds over them.

Mrs. Montague marveled at the exquisite fairness of her skin, and told herself that she had never realized, until that moment, how very beautiful her young seamstress was.

"You must put everything on, even to the jewels that I shall wear," she said, bringing a large case from one of her trunks, and exhibiting an almost childish eagerness to get the full effect of her costume.

She opened the case, and taking a diamond necklace of great beauty and value from it, clasped it about the girl's milk-white neck. Then she fastened some fine solitaires in her small ears; three or four pins, each having a blazing stone for its head, were tucked amid the glossy braids of her hair, and two glittering snakes were wound about her beautifully rounded arms.

"Now for the fan, and you will be complete," cried Mrs. Montague, as she brought an exquisite affair composed of white ostrich tips, with a bird of Paradise nestling in its center, and handed it to Mona.

Then she stood off to admire the *tout ensemble*, and just at that moment there came a tap upon her door.

She went immediately to open it, and found her nephew standing outside.

"I've come for the money, Aunt Margie," he said. "I thought I'd better have it to-night, since I am going to town on the early train, and did not like to disturb you in the morning."

"Very well, I will get it for you, and I hope that Madame Millaise will have the mantle ready for you, for I must have it on Monday evening to throw over my shoulders after dancing," Mrs. Montague responded, as she turned back to get her purse.

She was on the point of closing the door, for she did not care to have her nephew know what was going on within the room. But Mr. Louis Hamblin was very keen. He knew from her manner that something unusual was occurring, and so he boldly pushed on after her, and entered the chamber before she was aware of his intention.

He stopped suddenly, however, the moment he had crossed the threshold, stricken with astonishment, as his glance rested upon Mona.

He had known that the girl was unusually lovely, but he was not quite prepared to see such a vision of beauty as now greeted his eyes.

"Jove! Aunt Marg, isn't she a stunner?" he cried, under his breath. "You won't see one at the ball Monday night that can hold a candle to her!"

Mona had flushed a vivid scarlet when he had so unceremoniously forced his way into the room; but at his bold compliment she turned haughtily away from his gaze with the air of an offended queen.

Her bearing, though full of scorn, was replete with grace and dignity, while the voluminous train of the rich dress made her slender form seem even taller and more regal than it really was.

Mrs. Montague had been no less impressed with the young girl's beauty, but it would have affected her no more than that of a wax figure would have done had no one else been present to remark it. Now, however, at Louis' high praise, a feeling of envy sprang up in her heart, and a frown of

Mrs. Georgie Sheldon

annoyance gathered on her brow.

"I wish you would go out, Louis," she said, sharply. "It is very rude of you to thus force yourself into my room."

"Come now, Aunt Marg, that's a good one, when all my life I have been in the habit of running in and out of your room, to do your bidding like a lackey," the young man retorted, mockingly. "But really this is an unexpected treat," he added, wickedly. "Miss Richards, in these fine togs, is the most beautiful woman that I have ever seen. And—'pon my word, Aunt Marg, I really believe she looks like—"

"Louis!" came in a sharp, warning cry from Mrs. Montague's lips, as she wheeled around upon him, her blazing eyes having a dangerous gleam in them.

"Like—a *picture* that I have seen somewhere," he quietly finished, but with a meaning smile and intonation. "How you do snap a fellow up, Aunt Margie! Here, give me the money, and I will clear out before another blast!"

Mrs. Montague handed him a roll of bills, telling him in an icy tone to be sure and get back as early as possible on Monday; and then, as he beat a retreat before her offended looks, she sharply shut the door upon him.

"Take off that dress!" she abruptly commanded of Mona.

Deeply wounded by her ungracious tone, as well as indignant at what had just occurred, the fair girl quickly divested herself of the costly apparel, and then, wishing the woman a quiet good-night, withdrew to her own room.

But nothing could make her very unhappy with the glad refrain that was continually ringing in her heart:

"Ray is coming! I shall see him!" she kept saying over and over. All other emotions were swallowed up in the joy of this, and she was soon sleeping the sweet, restful sleep of youth and dreaming of the one she loved.

But Mrs. Montague was terribly excited when she found herself alone.

"I should never have thought of it if Louis had not spoken, I was so absorbed in the costume," she muttered, as she stood in the middle of the floor and tried to compose herself. "I could almost swear that she was Mona come back to life. She looked almost exactly as she did that night in Paris—shall I ever forget it?—when I *told* her, and she drew herself up in that proud way; and *she* had a garnet dress on, too. She *does* look wonderfully like that picture! Louis was quick to see it, and I will have it destroyed when I return to New York. I can't imagine why I have kept it all these years. Ugh! I feel almost as if I had seen a ghost."

She shook herself, as if to dispel these uncanny thoughts, and then disrobing, retired to rest.

Sunday was a lovely day—more mild and spring-like even than the previous ones had been.

Some of the guests at Hazeldean went to Rhinebeck to attend the morning service, Mr. Palmer and Mrs. Montague among the number; but most of them remained within doors until evening, when Mr. Wellington, their host, requested, as a favor, that all would attend a special service at one of the village churches, where a college friend was to preach, and he wished to give him as large an audience as possible. He also hinted, with a gleam of mischief in his eyes, that they would do well to take their pocket-books along, as a collection would be taken to help to pay for a new organ which the society had just purchased.

It was a glorious evening, and, everybody appearing to partake of the enthusiasm of the host, the whole party set out to walk to the church.

No one thought of asking Mona to go, and thus the young girl was left entirely alone in the house, except for the servants, who were by themselves in the basement.

She was very lonely, and felt both sad and depressed, as she saw the party pass out of sight down the avenue, and for a moment she was tempted to rebel against her hard lot, and the neglect of others, who might at least have remembered that she had a soul to be benefited by Sabbath services as well as they.

She even shed a few tears of regret, for she was young and buoyant, and would dearly have loved to join that gay company of youths and maidens, if she could have done so as an equal.

But after a few moments she bravely wiped away the crystal drops, saying:

"I will not grieve; I will not give up to *anything* until I have seen Ray. If *he* is true, the world will be bright, though everybody else gives me the cold shoulder—and he will be here to-morrow. But I *am* a trifle lonely, all by myself in this great house. I believe I will run down to the music-room and play for a little while. No one is here to be disturbed by it, and I shall not be afraid of critics."

So she went slowly down the dimly lighted stairs to a room on the right of the hall, where, without even turning up the gas, she seated herself at the piano.

The "dim religious light" was rather pleasant to her, in her tender mood, and she could see well enough for her purpose.

She ran her skilled fingers lightly over the keys of the sweet-toned instrument, and almost immediately her whole soul began to wake up to the rich harmony which she evoked.

She played a few selections from Beethoven's "Songs Without Words," sang a ballad or two, and was just upon the point of getting up to look for a book of Sabbath hymns, when a step behind her caused her to turn to ascertain who was intruding upon her solitude.

She saw standing in the doorway leading from the hall, a tall form clad in a long overcoat and holding his hat in his hand.

She could not distinguish his features, but courteously arose to go forward to see who the stranger was, when he spoke, and his tones thrilled her instantly to the very center of her being.

"Pardon me," he began. "I rang the bell, but no one answered it, and, the door being ajar, I ventured to enter. Can you tell me—Ah!—*Mona*!"

The speaker had also advanced into the room as he spoke, but the light was too dim for him to recognize its occupant until he reached her side, although she had known him the instant he spoke.

His start and exclamation of surprise, the glad, almost exultant tone as he uttered her name, told the fair girl all she needed to know to prove that Ray Palmer was loyal to her, in spite of all the reverses of fortune, of friends, of position, and to prove him the noble character she had always believed him to be.

Mrs. Georgie Sheldon

He stretched forth an eager hand, and grasped hers with a fervor which told her how deeply he was moved to find her, even before his words confirmed it.

"Oh! I *have* not made a mistake, have I?" he asked, bending his luminous face closer to hers, eager to read a welcome there. "I *have* found you—*at last*? If you knew—if I could tell you—But first tell *me* that you are glad to see me," he concluded, somewhat incoherently.

Mona's hand lay unresisting in his clasp, and a feeling of restful peace filled her heart, as she lifted her glad face to him.

"No, you have made no mistake—it is I, Mona Montague, and I am very"—with a little sob of joy, which she could not control—"very glad to see you again, Mr. Palmer."

"My darling!" he said, made bold by her look, her tone, but more by the little sob, which his own heart told him how to interpret. "Tell me yet more—I cannot wait—I have been so hungry for the sight of your dear face, for the sound of your voice, and I thought that I had lost you. I love you, Mona, with all my heart and strength, and this unexpected meeting has so overcome me that the truth must be told. Are you still 'glad'?—will you make *me* glad by telling me so?"

"But—Mr. Palmer—" Mona began, tremulously, hardly able to credit her ears, hardly able to believe that this great and almost overwhelming joy was a reality, and not some illusive dream. "I am afraid you forget—"

"What have I forgotten?" he gently asked, but without releasing her hand.

"That my uncle is gone. I have no home, friends, position!

Do you know—"

"I know that you are Mona Montague—that I *love* you, and that I have *found* you," he interrupted, his own voice quivering with repressed emotion, his strong frame trembling with eager longing, mingled with something of fear that his suit might be rejected.

"Then I *am* glad," breathed Mona, and the next moment she was folded close to Raymond Palmer's manly bosom, where she could feel the beating of the strong, true, loyal heart of her lover while with his lips pressed upon her silken hair he murmured fond words which betrayed how deep and absorbing his affection was for her—how he had longed for her and how bitterly he had suffered because he could not find her.

Mrs. Georgie Sheldon

CHAPTER XIX

MONA IS JOYFULLY SURPRISED

"Then you do love me, Mona?" Ray whispered, fondly, after a moment or two of happy silence. "I must hear you say it even though you have tacitly confessed it and my heart exults in the knowledge. I cannot be quite satisfied until I have the blessed confirmation from your own lips."

"You certainly can have no reason to doubt it after such a betrayal as this," Mona tried to say playfully, to shield her embarrassment, as she lifted her flushed face from its resting-place, and shot a glad, bright look into his eyes. Then she added in a grave though scarcely audible voice: "Yes I *do* love you with all my heart!"

The young man smiled; then with his arm still infolding her he led her beneath the chandelier and turned on a full blaze of light.

"I must read the glad story in your eyes," he said, tenderly, as he bent to look into them. "I must see it shining in your face. Ah, love, how beautiful you are still! And yet there is a sad droop to these lips"—and he touched them softly with his own—"that pains me; there is a heaviness about these eyes which tells of trial and sorrow. My darling, you have needed comfort and sympathy, while I was bound hand and foot, and could not come to you. What did you think of me, dear? But you knew, of course."

"I knew—I hoped there was some good reason," faltered Mona, with downcast eyes.

"You 'hoped!' Then you *did* think—you *feared* that I, like other false friends, had turned the cold shoulder on you in your trouble?" he returned, a sorrowful reproach in his tone. "Surely you have known about the stolen diamonds?"

"Yes, I knew that your father had been robbed."

"And about my having been kidnapped also—the papers were full of the story."

Mona looked up, astonished.

"Kidnapped!" she exclaimed. "No; this is the first that I have heard of that."

"Where have you been that you have not seen the papers?" Ray inquired, wonderingly.

"As you doubtless know," Mona replied, "Uncle Walter died very suddenly the day after I attended the opera with you, and for a fortnight afterward I was so overcome with grief and—other troubles, that I scarcely looked at a paper. After that, one day, I saw a brief item referring to the robbery, and it is only since I came here that I had even a hint that you had been ill."

"Come, then, dear, and let me tell you about it, and then I am sure you will absolve me from all willful neglect," Ray said, as he led her to a *tete-a-tete* and seated himself beside her.

"But first tell me," he added, "how I happen to find you here. Are you one of the guests?"

"No," Mona said, blushing slightly, "You know, of course, that I lost home and everything else when I lost Uncle Walter, and now I am simply acting as seamstress and waiting maid to a Mrs. Montague, who is a guest here."

"Ah!" exclaimed the young man, with a start, as he remembered how Mrs. Montague had denied all knowledge of Mona. "I have met the lady—is she a relative of yours?"

"No; at least, I never saw her until I entered her house to serve her."

"My poor child! to think that you should have to go out to do such work," said Ray, with tender regret. "But of course, as you say, I can understand all about it, for that, too, was in the papers; but it was very heartless, very cruel in that Mrs. Dinsmore not to make you any allowance, when she could not fail to know that your uncle wished you to inherit his property. She must be a very obnoxious sort of person, isn't she?"

"I do not know," said Mona, with a sigh; "I have never seen her—at least, not since I was a child, and too young to remember anything about her."

"Do you mean that you did not meet her during the contest for Mr. Dinsmore's fortune?" questioned Ray in surprise.

"No, she did not appear at all personally; all her business was transacted through her lawyer, as mine was through Mr. Graves," Mona answered.

"Well, it was an inhuman thing for her to do, to take

everything and leave you penniless, and obliged to earn your own living. But that is all over now," the young man said, looking fondly into the fair face beside him. "Isn't it, darling? You have told me that you love me, but you have not yet promised me anything. You are going to be my wife, are you not, Mona?"

"I hope so—if you wish—some time," she answered, naively, yet with crimson cheeks and downcast eyes.

He laughed out gladly as he again embraced her.

"'Some time, if I wish,'" he repeated. "Well, I do wish, and the some time must be very soon, too. Ah, my sweet, brown-eyed girlie! how happy I am at this moment! I did not dream that I was to find such a wealth of joy when I came hither at my father's earnest request. I was grieving so for you I had no heart for the gayeties which I knew I should find here; now, however, I shall not find it difficult to be as gay as any one. How glad I am, too, that I came to-night to find you here alone. My father does not expect me until to-morrow; but I had a matter of importance to talk over with him, so ran up on the evening train. But I am forgetting that I have a thrilling story to tell you."

He then related all that had occurred in connection with the bold diamond robbery and his imprisonment and subsequent illness in Doctor Wesselhoff's retreat for nervous patients, while Mona listened with wonder-wide eyes and a paling cheek, as she realized the danger through which her lover had passed.

"What an audacious scheme!" she exclaimed, when he concluded. "How could any woman dare to plan, much less put it into execution! No wonder that you were ill, and you must have been very sick, for you are still thin and pale,"

Mrs. Georgie Sheldon

Mona said, regarding him anxiously.

"I shall now soon outgrow that," Ray responded, smiling. "It was chiefly anxiety and unhappiness on your account that kept me thin and pale. You will see how quickly I shall recover my normal condition now that I have found you and know that you are all my own. Now tell me all about your own troubles, my darling. Do you know, it seems an age to me since we parted that night at your uncle's door, and you gave me permission to call upon you? My intention then was to seek an interview with Mr. Dinsmore within a day or two, tell him of my love for you, and ask his permission to address you. But, even had no misfortune overtaken me, I could not have done so, since he was stricken that very night; but at least I could have come to you with words of sympathy."

Mona then gave him a detailed account of all that had happened during those dark days, when her only friend lay dead and she felt as if all the world had forsaken her.

"Mona," the young man gravely said, when she had finished her story, "I shall tell my father to-night of this interview— he already knows that I love you—and ask his sanction to our immediate marriage, for I cannot have you remain here among my friends and acquaintances another day in the capacity of a seamstress or waiting-maid."

"But, Ray—" Mona began, then she stopped short, blushing rosily at having thus involuntarily called him by his Christian name. She had always thought of him thus, and it passed her lips before she was aware of it.

He laughed out, amused at her confusion.

"There, dear, you have broken the ice almost without

knowing it," he said; "now we shall get on nicely if you do not let it freeze over again; but what were you going to say?"

"I was going to ask you not to speak of—of our relations to each other to any one just yet," Mona returned, with some embarrassment.

"Why not?" Ray demanded, astonished, and looking troubled by the request.

"There are reasons why I must remain for a while longer with Mrs. Montague," said the young girl.

"Not in the capacity of waiting-maid," Ray asserted, decidedly; "I cannot allow that."

"Indeed I must, Ray," Mona persisted, but with an appealing note in her voice; "and I will tell you why. I told you that Mrs. Montague was no relative; she is not really, and yet—she was my father's second wife."

"Mona! you astonish me," cried her lover, regarding her wonderingly.

"It is true, and there is some mystery connected with my own mother and my early history which I am exceedingly anxious to learn. Uncle Walter told me something of it only the day before he died; but I am very sure that he kept back certain portions of the story which I ought to know, and which he was also anxious to tell me when he was dying, and could not. I have no means even of proving my identity; if I had, I suppose that I could claim some of this wealth of which Mrs. Montague appears to have abundance, and I am sure that she has some proof in her possession. I want to get it, and that is why I am anxious to remain with her a little longer. Let me tell you everything," Mona went on, hurriedly, as Ray seemed about to utter another protest to her wish. "As I understand the story, my father was dependent upon a rich aunt who wished him to marry the present Mrs. Montague; but he, being in love with my mother, was opposed to so doing, although he was anxious to secure the fortune. As he was about to start on a European tour he married my mother and took her with him, none of his friends apparently suspecting the union.

"Now comes a part of the story which I cannot understand. They traveled for several months; but, while in Paris, my father suddenly disappeared, and my mother, believing herself deserted, in her pride and humiliation, immediately left the city, doubtless with the intention of returning to America. She was taken ill in London, however, and there, a few months later, I was born, and she died only a few hours afterward. Uncle Walter heard of her sad condition, and hastened to her, but was three days too late, and found only a poor weak infant upon whom to expend his love and care. It seems very strange to me that she did not write to him at the time she fled from Paris; but I suppose, since she had eloped with and been secretly married to my father, she was too proud and sensitive to appeal to any one. Later, my father married this Miss Barton to please his aunt and secure the fortune which he so much desired. I do not know anything about his after-life. I questioned Uncle Walter, but he would not talk about him—the most that he would tell me was that he was dead, but how, or when he died, I could never learn, and I do not know as there even exists any proof of his legal marriage with my mother, although my uncle confidentially asserted that she was his lawful wife. I believe, however, that such proofs do exist and that they are in Mrs. Montague's possession."

Mona then proceeded to relate how she had happened to secure the position she now occupied.

"It seems very strange," she said, "that fate should have thrown me thus into her home, and somehow I have a suspicion that she must have been concerned in the great wrong done my mother—that it was because of her influence that my father never owned nor provided for me. And now," Mona continued, flushing a deep crimson, "I am obliged to confess something of which I am somewhat ashamed. When I found myself in Mrs. Montague's home, and had resolved to remain, I knew that she would instantly suspect my identity if I should give her my true name. This, of course, I did not wish her to do, and so when she asked me what she should call me, I told her 'Ruth Richards,' The name Ruth really belongs to me, but Richards is assumed. Now, Ray, you can understand why I do not wish to have Mrs. Montague undeceived regarding my identity, as she must be if you insist upon at once proclaiming our relations. I am very strongly impressed that she knows the secret of my father's desertion of my mother, and also that she could prove, if she would, that I am the child of their legal marriage."

Ray Palmer had grown very grave while listening to Mona's story, and when she spoke of her assumed name it was evident, from the frown on his brow, that he did not approve of having her hide herself from the world in any such way.

"Why not ask her outright, then?" inquired this straight-forward young man, as the young girl concluded.

"That would never do at all," said Mona. "Uncle Walter told me that she hated my mother, and me a hundred-fold on her account, and she would not be very likely to put any proofs into my hands, especially when they would be liable to be very detrimental to her own interests."

"True, I did not think of that," returned Ray, thoughtfully. "But how do you expect to obtain possession of these proofs,

Mrs. Georgie Sheldon

even if she has them, and how long must I wait for you?" he gloomily added.

"I do not know, Ray,' she answered, with a sigh. "I do not see my way very clearly. I keep hoping, and something seems to hold me to this position in spite of myself. Let me remain three or six months longer; then if I do not succeed—"

"I will concede three months, but no more," Ray interposed, decidedly; then added: "What does it matter whether you know all this history or not? It cannot be anything of vital importance, or that will affect your future in any way. I wish you would let me speak to my father and announce our engagement at once, my darling."

"Nay, please, Ray, let me have my way in this," Mona pleaded, with crimson cheeks. She could not tell him that she felt sensitive about becoming his wife until she could have absolute proof of the legal marriage of her father and mother.

He bent down and looked earnestly into her face.

"Mona, is that the only reason why you wish to wait? You do not shrink from our union from any doubt of your own heart—of your love for me, or mine for you?" he gravely asked.

"No, indeed, Ray," and she put out both her hands to him, with an eagerness that entirely reassured him even before she added: "I cannot tell you how glad, how restful, how content I am since your coming to-night. I was so lonely and sorrowful, the future looked so dark and cheerless because I feared I had lost you; but now all is bright."

She dropped her face again upon his breast to hide the blushes this confession had called up, and the happy tears also that were dropping from her long lashes.

He gathered her close to his heart, thrilling at her words.

"Then I will try to be patient for three months, love," he murmured, "and meantime I suppose you will have to be Ruth Richards to me as well as to others."

"Yes, it will not do to have my real name known—that will spoil all," Mona replied, with a sigh, for her truthful soul recoiled with as much aversion from all deception as he possibly could do.

"And am I not to see you during all this time?" Ray ruefully asked.

"Oh, yes; not to see you would be unbearable to me," Mona responded quickly. "Can you not manage to have some one introduce me to you as Miss Richards while you are here? then neither Mrs. Montague nor any one else would think it strange if you should seek me occasionally; only—"

"Only what?" inquired the young man, wondering to see her color so vividly and appear so embarrassed.

"Perhaps I should not tell you," Mona said, with some hesitation, "and yet you must learn the fact sooner or later from some other sources; but Mrs. Montague appears to be growing quite fond of your father, who is very attentive to her, and she might not exactly like—"

"She might not like to have the son of the man for whom she is angling to pay attention to her seamstress, is what you were going to say?" Ray interposed, laughing, yet with a look of annoyance sweeping over his fine face.

"Something like it, perhaps," Mona responded, flushing again.

"Well, I do not believe she is going to land her fish, if you will pardon the slang phrase," said the young man, confidently. "My father has successfully resisted the allurements of the gentler sex for too many years to succumb at this late day; so you and I need give ourselves no uneasiness upon that score. Does he know you as Ruth Richards?"

"Yes, if indeed he knows me at all. I have received no introduction to him, and I only knew him from hearing Mr. Wellington greet him and inquire regarding the lost diamonds," Mona explained. Then she added: "Do you expect to recover them, Ray? have you any clew?"

"Yes, we have a slight one, we think, and that is one reason why I am here to-night. The detective in our employ sent a telegram to my father yesterday mentioning the fact, but he thought it best for me to come up to-night and talk the matter over more fully with him, and hurry him back to New York early on Tuesday morning. A woman is being shadowed upon the suspicion of having committed a bold swindle in Chicago, and Mr. Rider thinks, without any doubt, that she is the same person who so cleverly did us out of our diamonds."

"Hark! please," said Mona, as just then she caught the sound of voices in the distance, "the party is returning from evening service, and I must not be found here with you."

"I am loath to let you go, my brown-eyed sweetheart," Ray tenderly responded.

"And I to go," Mona answered softly, "but it is best that I should; we must both be judicious for a while—we must not be too exacting when we have had this great new happiness come to us so unexpectedly," and she lifted her luminous eyes to him.

He clasped her to him again.

"Good-night, my darling," he said; then with one lingering kiss upon her lips, he let her go, and she stole softly up stairs, with a joyous heart and step, while Ray drew a paper from his pocket, and was apparently deeply absorbed in its contents when the party entered the house.

A good deal of surprise was expressed when his arrival was discovered, and he was accorded a warm welcome by the host and hostess as well as by every guest.

Mrs. Georgie Sheldon

CHAPTER XX

MR. RIDER MAKES AN ARREST

While the festivities were in progress at Hazeldean, some incidents of a somewhat singular character were occurring in New York.

It will be remembered that Mr. Palmer and his son met Mrs. Montague for the first time at the reception given by Mrs. Merrill; also that their attention was attracted to a lady who wore a profusion of unusually fine diamonds—a Mrs. Vanderheck.

We know how Ray was introduced to her, and repeated her name as Vander*beck*, with an emphasis on the beck; how she started, changed color, and glanced at him curiously as he did so, and seemed strangely ill at ease while conversing with him afterward, and a little later abruptly took her leave.

The next day, the young man communicated these suspicious circumstances to the private detective whom his father had employed to look up his stolen diamonds, and from that time Mrs. Vanderheck had been under close surveillance by that shrewd official.

Mr. Rider was a very energetic man, and, by dint of adroit

inquiries and observations, learned that she was a woman who devoted most of her time to social life—was very gay, very fond of dress and excitement of every kind. She did not, however, resemble in any way the Mrs. Vanderbeck who had conducted the robbery of the Palmer diamonds, although, he argued, she might easily enough be an accomplice.

The detective interviewed Doctor Wesselhoff, who was now as eager as any one to assist in the discovery of those who so imposed upon him, and obtained a minute description of the other woman who had arranged for Ray Palmer to become an inmate of his institution, and he thought that possibly by the aid of a clever disguise, Mrs. Vanderheck might have figured as Mrs. Walton, the pretended mother of the pretended monomaniac.

Consequently, energetic Mr. Rider had followed close upon her track, bound to discover her real character.

She resided in a fine brown-stone mansion up town; sported an elegant carriage and a spanking pair of bays, and, to all appearances, possessed an unlimited bank account.

She was sometimes attended on her drives by a gentleman, many years older than herself, who appeared to be something of an invalid, and who, as far as the detective could learn, was engaged in no business whatever.

These latter facts increased his suspicions, for the reason that the woman who had robbed Mr. Palmer had wished to submit her selections to the sanction of an invalid husband.

Disguised as a spruce young coachman, Mr. Rider managed to ingratiate himself with a pretty, but rather vain young servant-girl in Mrs. Vanderheck's employ, and by means of well-turned compliments, re-enforced now and then with some pretty gift, he managed to keep himself well posted regarding the mistress' movements and her social engagements, and then he diligently followed up his espionage by frequenting the many receptions and balls which she attended.

At these places she was always magnificently attired and seldom wore any ornaments except diamonds, of which she appeared to possess an endless store, and all were of great beauty and value.

It was at a Delmonico ball, which was given in honor of a person of royal descent, and on the Friday evening preceding Ray Palmer's visit to Hazeldean, that Mr. Rider found his plans ripe for action and accomplished his great *coup de grace*.

He had learned, through the pretty servant-girl, that Mrs. Vanderheck was to grace the occasion with her presence and was to be attired in a costume of unusual richness and elegance—"with diamonds enough to blind you," the lively and voluble Fanny had boasted to her admirer.

Consequently the detective got himself up in elaborate style, obtained a ticket for the ball by some means best known to himself, and, when the festivities were at their height, slipped in upon the brilliant scene.

He was not long in "spotting" his prey, who was conspicuous in white brocaded velvet and white ostrich tips, while her person was literally ablaze with diamonds.

"Great Scott!" the man muttered, as he ran his keen eye over her gorgeous attire; "it is a mystery to me how any woman dare wear such a fortune upon her person; she is liable to be murdered any day. Why, she—Aha!"

His heart gave a sudden leap, and for a moment, as he afterward described his sensations, it seemed as if some one had struck him on the head with a club, for he actually saw stars and grew so dizzy and confused that he could scarcely stand; for—*in the woman's ears he caught sight of a gleaming pair of crescents*!

He soon recovered himself, however, and took a second look. He had, as we know, been looking for those peculiar ornaments for more than three years, and now he had found them, as he had always believed he should, upon a gay woman of fashion in the midst of fashionable admirers.

It did not take him long to decide upon his course of action, and he was now again the cool and collected detective, although the fierce glitter in his eyes betrayed some relentless purpose in his mind.

He made his way quietly into a corner, where he stood covertly watching the brilliant woman, and comparing her appearance with a description that was written in cipher upon some tablets which he took from his pocket.

"'Very attractive, about twenty-eight or thirty years, rather above medium height, somewhat inclined toward *embonpoint*, fair complexion, blue eyes, short, curling red hair,'—Hum!" he softly interposed at this point, "she answers very well to all except the red hair; but drop a red wig over her light-colored pate, tint her eyebrows and lashes with the same color, and I'll wager my badge against a last year's hat we'd have the Bently widow complete. There can be no doubt about the crescents, though, and that cross on her bosom looks wonderfully like the one that Palmer described to me. I suppose she thought no one would be on the lookout for it here, and she could safely wear it with all the rest, I always said the same woman put up both jobs," he

Mrs. Georgie Sheldon

interposed, with a satisfied chuckle. "Guess I'll take a nearer look at the stones, though, before I do anything desperate."

He put up his tablets, and began to move slowly about the rooms; but his eagle eye never once left the form of the woman in white brocaded velvet.

Three hours later, Mrs. Vanderheck, wrapped in an elegant circular of crimson satin, bordered with ermine, and attended by her maid and a dignified policeman as a body-guard, swept down the grand stair-way leading from the ball-room to the street, on her way to her carriage.

As she stepped out across the pavement and was about to enter the vehicle, a quiet, gentlemanly looking person approached her and saluted her respectfully.

"Madame—Mrs. Vander*beck*," with an intentional emphasis on the last syllable, "you are my prisoner!"

The woman gave a violent start as she caught the name, and darted a keen glance of inquiry at him, all of which Mr. Rider was quick to note.

Then she drew herself up haughtily.

"Sir, I do not know you, and my name is not Vander*beck*; you have made a mistake," she said, icily.

"I have made no mistake. You are the woman I have been looking for, for more than three years, whether you spell your name with a *b*, an *h*, or in a different way altogether; and I repeat—you are my prisoner."

Mr. Rider laid his hand firmly but respectfully on her arm, as he ceased speaking, to enforce his meaning.

She shook him off impatiently.

"What is the meaning of this strange proceeding?" she demanded, indignantly; then turning to the policeman who attended her, she continued, in a voice of command: "I appeal to you for protection against such insolence."

"How is this, Rider?" now inquired the officer, who recognized the detective, and was astonished beyond measure by this unexpected arrest.

"She has on her person diamonds that I have been looking for, for over three years, and I cannot afford to let them slip through my fingers after such a hunt as that," the detective quietly explained.

"It is false!" the woman stoutly and indignantly asserted. "I wear no jewelry that is not my own property. Everything I have was either given to me or purchased with my husband's money."

"I trust you will be able to prove the truth of your assertions, madame," Mr. Rider quietly returned. "If you can do so, you will, of course, have no further trouble. But I must do my duty. I have been employed to search for a pair of diamond crescents which properly belong to a person in Chicago. I have seen such a pair in your ears to-night. You also wear a cross like one that I am searching for, and I shall be obliged to take you into custody until the matter can be properly investigated."

Mrs. Vanderheck was evidently very much startled and upset by this information, yet she behaved with remarkable fortitude, considering the trying circumstances.

"What am I to do?" she inquired, again appealing to the

policeman attending her. "The crescents he mentions are *mine*—I bought them almost three years ago in Boston. Of course, I know that I must prove my statement, and I think I can if you will give me time, for I believe I still have the bill of sale in my possession. I will look it up, and if"—turning to the detective—"you will call upon me some time to-morrow you shall have it."

Mr. Rider smiled, for the unsophisticated suggestion amused him immensely.

"I cannot lose sight of you, madame," he said, courteously. "What you have said may be true; I shall be glad, on your account, if it proves so; but my duty to others must be rigidly enforced, and so I am obliged to arrest you."

"But *I* cannot submit to an *arrest*; you surely do not mean that I—a woman in *my* position—am to be imprisoned on the charge of *theft*!" exclaimed the woman, growing deadly white.

"The law is no respecter of persons or position, madame," laconically responded the detective.

"What *can I* do?' Mrs. Vanderheck cried, in a tone of despair.

"Rider, I am afraid you have made a mistake," the policeman now remarked, in a low tone; "the woman is all right. I've acted as escort for her on such occasions as these for the last two years."

The detective looked astonished and somewhat perplexed at this statement.

If Mrs. Vanderheck had led a respectable life in New York

for two years, and was as well known to this officer as he represented, he also began to fear that he might have made a mistake.

"You are willing to defer the arrest if she can furnish ample security for her appearance when wanted?" the policeman asked, after a moment of thought.

"Ye-es; but responsible parties must vouch for her," Mr. Rider answered, with some hesitation.

The woman seized the suggestion with avidity.

"Oh, then, I have a dozen friends who will serve me," she cried, eagerly. "Come back to the ball-room with me and you shall have security to any amount." and with a haughty air she turned back and entered the brilliantly lighted building which she had recently left.

The policeman conducted them into a small reception-room, and Mrs. Vanderheck sent her card, with a few lines penciled on it, to a well-known banker, who was among the guests in the ball-room, requesting a few moments' personal conversation with him.

The gentleman soon made his appearance, and was greatly astonished and no less indignant upon being informed of what had occurred.

But he readily understood that the matter in hand must be legally settled before the lady could be fully acquitted. He therefore unhesitatingly gave security for her to the amount required by the detective, but politely refused to receive, as a guarantee of her integrity, the costly ornaments which Mrs. Vanderheck offered him then and there for the service so kindly rendered.

She, then, without a murmur, delivered over to the detective, in the presence of her friend, the policeman, and her maid, the contested crescents and cross, and was then allowed to take her departure, with her attendants, without further ceremony.

Early the next morning the following message went flashing over the Western wires to Chicago, addressed thus:

"To JUSTIN CUTLER, ESQ.:—Crescents found. Come at once to identify. Bring bogus ones.

"RIDER."

The detective then sought Mr. Palmer, but upon being informed that he was out of town, and would not return until the early part of the coming week, he related to Ray what had happened on the previous evening, and advised him to communicate the fact as soon as possible, to his father, and notify him that an examination would take place at ten o'clock on the following Tuesday.

Ray had already telegraphed, in answer to his father's message, that he would come to Hazeldean on Monday for the ball, and at first he thought he would make no change in his plans. The news was good news, and would keep for a day or two, he told himself.

But the detective's enthusiasm over the arrest was so contagious, he found himself wishing that his father could also know what had occurred.

He had an engagement for that evening—which was Saturday—so he could not go to Hazeldean that day, and finally contented himself by commissioning Mr. Rider to drop Mr. Palmer a message, giving him a hint of the arrest, and then arranged to go himself to explain more fully, by the Sunday evening train.

It almost seemed as if fate had purposely arranged it thus, that he might find Mona alone as he did, to declare his love, and win in return the confession of her affection for him.

The moment his father entered the house and met him, on his return from the evening service at the village, he realized that some great change had come over him; he was very different from the depressed, anxious-eyed son whom he had left only a few days previous.

He could hardly attribute it entirely to the news of the arrest of the supposed thief of the diamonds, and yet he could think of nothing else, for he firmly believed that Walter Dinsmore's niece had left New York after her uncle's death, and he had no reason to believe that Ray had found trace of her.

But whatever had caused the change—whatever had served to bring back the old light to his eyes, the old smile to his lips, and all his former brightness and energy of manner, he was grateful for it, and he hailed the result with a delight that made itself manifest in the hearty grip of his hand and his eager-toned:

"How are you, Ray, my boy? I am glad to see you."

Mrs. Georgie Sheldon

CHAPTER XXI

MONA AND RAY HAVE ANOTHER INTERVIEW

Mona was very happy as she went up to her room after her interview with Ray that eventful Sunday evening, during the early part of which life had seemed darker than usual to her.

The man whom she loved was true, in spite of the doubt and sorrow she had experienced over his apparent neglect. She had not after all built her hopes upon shifting sand; she had not reared an idol in her heart only to have to hurl it from its shrine as false and worthless. Oh, no; her lover was a man to be reverenced—to be proud of, and to be trusted under all circumstances.

She exulted in these facts almost as much as in the knowledge of his love for her, and she dropped to sleep with joy in her heart, smiles on her lips, and tears of gratitude flashing like diamonds on her long brown lashes.

The next morning she seemed almost like a new creature. The world had suddenly acquired a wonderful brightness and beauty, and it was a delight even to exist.

It was no hardship to be a seamstress or even a waiting-maid, so long as she was blessed with Raymond Palmer's love and with the prospect of becoming his wife in the near future.

Involuntarily a gay little song rippled from her lips while she was dressing, and the unusual sound catching Mrs. Montague's ear caused a look of surprise to sweep over her face, for she had never heard Ruth Richards sing so much as a note before.

"The girl has a sweet, flexible voice. I wonder if she is going to surprise me, every now and then, with some new accomplishment! Maybe I have an embryo *prima-donna* in my employ!" she muttered, with a scornful smile.

Her surprise was not diminished when she saw the happy girl with her bright and animated manners and the new love-light shining on her face, making it almost dazzling in its intensified loveliness.

"What has come over you, Ruth?" Mrs. Montague inquired, regarding her curiously. "One would almost imagine you were going to the ball yourself to-night, you appear to be so happy and elated."

"I believe there must be something unusually exhilarating in the atmosphere," Mona replied, a gleeful little laugh rippling over her smiling lips, although she blushed beneath the woman's searching look. "Don't you think that excitement is sometimes infectious?—and surely everybody has been active and gay for days. I like to see people happy, and then the morning is perfectly lovely."

Truly the world was all *couleur de rose* to her since love's elixir had given a new impetus to her heart-pulses!

Mrs. Montague frowned slightly, for somehow the girl's unusual mood annoyed her.

Mrs. Georgie Sheldon

She could not forget her exceeding loveliness on Saturday evening, when she had been arrayed in the festal robe which she herself was to wear at the ball, and the memory of it nettled her.

Perhaps, she thought, Ruth remembered it also, and was secretly exulting over the fact of her own beauty. Exceedingly vain herself, she was quick to suspect vanity in others, and this thought only increased her irritation.

"I'd give a great deal if she wasn't so pretty; and—and that style of beauty always annoys me," she said to herself, with a feeling of angry impatience.

And giving a sudden twitch to a delicate ruffle, which she had begun to arrange upon the corsage of a dress, to show Mona how she wanted it, she made a great rugged tear in the filmy fabric, thus completely ruining the frill.

This only served to increase her ill humor.

"There! now I cannot wear this dress at dinner to-day," she cried, flushing angrily over the mishap, "for the frill is ruined."

"Haven't you something else that you can use in its place?" Mona quietly asked.

"No; nothing looks as well on this corsage as these wide, fleecy frills of *crape lisse*. It is the only dress, too, that I have not already worn here, and I was depending upon it for to-day," was the irritable response.

Mona thought she had plenty of laces and ruffles that would have answered very well, and which might easily have been substituted, but she did not think it best to make any further suggestions to her in her present mood.

"I know what I can do," Mrs. Montague continued, after a moment, in a milder tone. "I saw some ruffling very nearly like this in a milliner's window at Rhinebeck, when I was out riding on Saturday. There are some other little things that I shall want for this evening, and you may take a walk by and by to get them for me."

Rhinebeck was a full mile away, and Mrs. Montague could easily have arranged to have Mona ride, for a carriage was sent every morning for the mail; but it did not occur to her to do so, or if it did, she evidently did not care to put herself to that trouble.

Mona, however, did not mind the walk—indeed, on the whole, she was rather glad of the privilege of getting out by herself into the sunshine which was so in harmony with her own bright mood. Still she could not help feeling that it was rather inconsiderate of Mrs. Montague to require her to walk two miles simply to gratify a mere whim.

It was about nine o'clock when she started out upon her errand, and as she ran down the steps and out upon the broad avenue, her bright eyes went glancing eagerly about, for Mona had secretly hoped that she might catch a glimpse of and perhaps even secure a few words with her lover.

But Ray was nowhere visible, being just at that moment in the smoking-room with several other gentlemen.

Mr. Palmer, the senior, however, was walking in the park, and evidently deeply absorbed in the consideration of some important matter, for his hands were clasped behind him, his head was bowed, and his eyes fixed upon the ground.

Mrs. Georgie Sheldon

But he glanced up as Mona passed him, and his eyes lighted as they fell upon her beautiful face.

He lifted his hat and bowed as courteously to her as he would have done to Mrs. Montague herself, and Mona's heart instantly warmed toward him for his politeness as she returned his salute.

"She is the prettiest girl in the house if she *is* only a waiting-maid," he muttered, as he turned for a second to look at the graceful figure after Mona had passed him. "How finely she carries herself—how elastic her step!"

Another pair of observing eyes had also caught sight of her by this time, and mental comments of a far different character were running through a younger brain.

The smoking-room at Hazeldean was in the third story of the south wing of the house, and overlooked the avenue and park, as well as a broad stretch of country beyond, and Ray Palmer, sitting beside one of the windows—apparently listening to the conversation of his companions, but really thinking of his interview with Mona the previous evening— espied his betrothed just as she was leaving the grounds of Hazeldean and turning into the main road.

He knocked the ashes from his cigar, took another whiff or two, then laid it down, and turned to his host, who was sitting near him.

"I believe I would like a canter across the country this bright morning, Mr. Wellington," he remarked. "May I beg the use of a horse and saddle for a couple of hours?"

"Certainly, Mr. Palmer—whatever I have in the stable in the form of horses or vehicles is as the disposal of my guests," was the courteous reply. "It is a fine morning for a ride," the gentleman added, "and perchance," with an arch smile, "you may be able to find some bright-eyed maiden who would be glad to accompany you."

Ray thanked him, and then hastened away to the stable to select his horse—his companion he knew he would find later on. In less than fifteen minutes from the time he had seen Mona leave the grounds he was cantering in the same direction; but she was a rapid walker, and he did not overtake her until she had nearly reached the village.

She caught the sound of a horse's hoofs behind her, but did not like to look back to see who was approaching, and it was only when the equestrian was close beside her that she glanced up to find the fond, smiling eyes of her lover resting upon her.

The glad look of welcome which leaped into her own eyes and flashed over her face told him how well he was beloved far better than any words could have done.

"*Ray*!" she exclaimed, in a joyous tone, as he drew rein beside her, and unhesitatingly laid her hand within the strong palm which he extended to her.

"My darling!" he returned, as he leaped to the ground, "this is an unexpected pleasure! I hardly dared to hope that I should see you alone to-day. How does it happen that you are so far from Hazeldean and walking?"

"Mrs. Montague had a few errands which she wished me to do for her in the village," Mona explained.

"Could she not have arranged for you to ride?" Ray asked, with a frown, and flushing to have his dear one's comfort so ignored.

"Oh, I do not mind the walk in the least," she hastened to say. "The morning is very lovely, and I am glad, on the whole, for I should have missed you if I had ridden."

"True, I saw you just as you were leaving Hazeldean, and so came after you," Ray returned, smiling.

They were just entering Rhinebeck now, and Mona looked anxiously up and down the street.

She feared that some of the other guests at Hazeldean might be about and see her with Ray if they should go through the place together.

He was quick to note the anxiety, and to understand its cause.

"How long will it take you to make your purchases, Mona?" he inquired, looking at his watch.

"Half an hour, perhaps," she replied.

"Well, then, I will leave you here, for a little trot about the country, and meet you again at this spot at the end of thirty minutes. I cannot resist the temptation to have a little chat with you on the way home," Ray returned, and, with another fond pressure of the hand, he leaped again upon his horse and galloped away.

With a rapidly beating heart and flushed cheeks, Mona hurried on her way. She made her purchases with all possible dispatch, then, as she had a few minutes to spare, she slipped into a hot-house, where flowers were cultivated for the city market, and bought a bunch of white violets, and a few sprays of heliotrope, then she turned her footsteps back toward Hazeldean.

She had hardly reached the spot where she had parted from Ray, when she heard him coming in the distance.

He joined her in another moment, and springing from the saddle, he threw the bridle-rein over his arm and walked beside her, leading his horse.

They had not proceeded far when they came to a place where another road appeared to branch off from the road they were on.

"Let us turn here," Ray said. "I have been exploring while you were in the village, and I found that this is a kind of lane, hedged on either side with a thick growth of pines, and leads back to the main road farther on. It is a little roundabout, but we shall not be likely to meet any one whom we know, and we shall feel far more freedom."

Mona was very glad to adopt this plan, and wandering slowly along beneath the shadows of the heavy pines, the lovers soon forgot that there was any one else in the world except themselves.

They talked over more fully the incidents of the weeks of their separation, but Ray dwelt a good deal upon the story of the stolen diamonds, and Mona could not fail to observe that he was very much troubled about the affair.

"It is a great loss," he remarked, with a sigh, "and though I cannot feel that I am culpably blamable, yet I do not cease to reproach myself for having been so thoroughly fooled by that woman. If I had only retained my hold upon the package, she never could have got it."

"But you may recover the diamonds, even now," Mona remarked. "You say that the detective arrested a woman on Friday evening as the suspected party."

"Yes, he suspects her in connection with another case, which he has been at work upon for over three years," and Ray related the story of the stolen crescents, then continued: "At the Delmonico ball he saw this Mrs. Vanderheck with them in her ears, and a cross like one that we lost, so he arrested her upon suspicion of both robberies, but somehow I am not very sanguine that we shall recover the stones."

"Did you not see the cross?" Mona asked.

"No; Mr. Rider had deposited it somewhere for safe keeping. It will be produced at the examination to-morrow. But, really, Mona," Ray interposed, with a nervous laugh, "I feel worse over the fact of having been so taken in by this pretended Mrs. Vanderbeck, than over the pecuniary loss."

The poor fellow felt very much as Justin Cutler felt when he learned how he had been tricked into paying a large price for the pair of paste crescents.

"How did the woman look, Ray? Describe her to me," Mora said.

She experienced a strange fascination in the story with all its curious details.

Ray gave a vivid word-picture of the beautiful woman, her dress, her carriage, and even her driver, for everything connected with that unexampled experience was indelibly stamped upon his mind.

"You say her dress was badly torn," Mona musingly observed,

when he had concluded the account of the discovery, and what had followed their getting out of the carriage and entering Doctor Wesselhoff's office.

"Yes, there was quite a rent in it, and I imagine this circumstance was not premeditated in the plan of her campaign, for she certainly was annoyed to have the beautiful cloth torn, although she tried to make light of it," Ray replied, then added: "And later in the day I found a piece of the goods adhering to my clothing."

"Did you?" questioned Mona, eagerly.

"Yes, and if I should ever see that dress again I could easily identify it, for I have the piece now and could fit it into the rent. But doubtless my lady has disposed of that costume long before this. Here is the piece, though—I have kept it, thinking it might possibly be of use some time."

Ray drew forth his pocket-book as he spoke, opened it, took out a folded paper, and handed it to Mona.

She opened it, and found carefully pinned within, a scrap of mauve colored ladies' cloth, in the form of a ragged acute angle.

"It is almost like broadcloth—very fine and heavy," she exclaimed. "It is a lovely color, too, and must have been a very beautiful costume."

"It was, and dangerously so," said Ray, dryly. "I admired it exceedingly, especially the fit and make of it."

"I imagine it might have been found in some dye-house shortly after, if you had only thought of it and known where to look," Mona thoughtfully observed.

"That is a bright idea," said Ray, quickly. "I honestly believe that women would make keener and better detectives than men. But," with a sigh, "I'm afraid it is too late now to put your theory to the test, and perhaps I have brushed against its folds on the street a dozen times since in a different color. Well, I suppose I must try to reconcile myself to the inevitable and make up my mind that the stones are gone beyond recovery, unless this Mrs. Vanderheck should prove to be the thief. I have not much faith in the detective's theory, that the Chicago adventuress and our diamond thief are one and the same."

"There seems to be a singular coincidence about the name of the lady who so imposed upon you, and that of the one who is now under arrest,' Mona remarked.

"Yes, the only difference is in one letter, and if Mrs. Vanderheck does not prove to be my charmer, or connected with her in any way, I shall be tempted to believe that she purposely took a name so similar in order to throw suspicion upon this woman," said the young man, thoughtfully.

"That may be; and is it not a little suspicious, too, that Mrs. Vanderbeck should have mentioned an invalid husband when Mrs. Vanderheck really has one?" Mona inquired.

"I had not thought of that before," Ray replied. "Still another singular circumstance comes to my mind just at this moment. At the time I was introduced to Mrs. Vanderheck, at Mrs. Merrill's reception, I repeated the name as if it was spelled with a 'b,' and emphasized the last syllable. The woman started, glanced at me curiously, and changed color a trifle, while she did not seem to quite recover her self-possession throughout our conversation."

"That does seem rather strange, considering all things," said

Mona. "Perhaps, after all, she may prove to be your adventuress; and yet she must be a very bold one to flaunt her plunder so recklessly and in the very presence of people who would be sure to recognize it."

They changed the subject after that, and chatted upon topics of a more tender and interesting nature.

It was a delightful walk in the mild February air, and a pleasant interview, and both were loath to part when they suddenly found themselves at the other end of the pine-shadowed lane where it curved into the main road again.

Ray took a tender leave of his dear one, then mounting his horse, rode back over the way they had just traversed, while Mona went on to Hazeldean.

CHAPTER XXII

MONA ATTENDS THE BALL AT HAZELDEAN

Mona found considerable excitement and confusion prevailing upon her return, for carpenters and decorators were busy about the house; flowers and plants were being carried in from the conservatory; the caterer and his force were arranging things to their minds, in the dining-room and kitchen, and everybody, guests included, was busy and in a flutter of anticipation over the approaching festivities.

"It seems to me that you were gone a long while," Mrs. Montague curtly remarked, as Mona entered her room.

"Was I?" the young girl asked, pleasantly; then she added: "Well, two miles make quite a walk."

Mrs. Montague flushed at the remark.

She was well aware that she had been unreasonable in requiring so much, just to secure a few articles which she might have very well done without, and this thought did not add to her comfort.

She made no reply, but quietly laid out some work for Mona, whom she kept busily employed during the remainder of the day.

The young girl cheerfully performed all that was required of her, however; her interview with Ray had served to sweeten every task for that day, while she hoped that she might secure another opportunity, before it was over, for a few more words with him.

But after dinner Mrs. Montague came up stairs better-natured than she had been all day, and turning to Mona, as she entered the room, she asked:

"Have you none but mourning dresses with you? nothing white, or pretty, for evening?"

"No; my dresses are all black; the only thing I have that would be at all suitable for evening is a black net," Mona answered, wondering, with rising color, why she had asked the question.

"That might do with some white ribbons to liven it up a bit," said Mrs. Montague, thoughtfully. Then she explained: "Mr. Wellington has arranged a balcony in the dancing hall for some friends who are coming to the ball, just to look on for a while, and he has just said to me that there would be a seat for you, if you cared to see the dancing."

Mona looked up eagerly at this.

She dearly loved social life, and she had wished, oh, so much! that she might have the privilege of witnessing the gay scenes of the evening.

"That is very kind of Mr. Wellington," she gratefully remarked.

"Get your dress, and let me look at it," continued Mrs. Montague, who would not commit herself to anything until she could be sure that her seamstress would make a respectable appearance among Mr. Wellington's friends.

He had requested as a favor that Miss Richards might be allowed this privilege in return for having so kindly relieved his daughter at the piano a few evenings previous.

Mona brought the dress—a rich, heavy net, made over handsome black silk, which had been among her wardrobe for the previous summer, when she went to Lenox with her uncle.

"That will be just the thing, only it needs something to relieve its blackness," said Mrs. Montague, while she mentally wondered at the richness of the costume.

"I have some narrow white taste in my trunk, which I can perhaps use to make it a little more suitable for the occasion, if you approve," Mona quietly remarked.

"Yes, fix it as you like," the lady returned, indifferently, adding: "that is if you care about going into the pavilion."

"Thank you; I think I should enjoy watching the dancers for a while," the young girl returned.

Perhaps, she thought, she might be able to snatch another brief interview with Ray. At all events she should see him, and that would be worth a great deal.

Her nimble fingers were very busy after that running her white ribbons into the meshes of her dress.

She wove three rows of the narrow, feather-edged taste into

each of the flounces, and the effect was very pretty. Then she did the same between the puffs of the full sleeves, tying some dainty bows where she joined them, and finished the neck to correspond.

This was hardly completed when she was called to assist Mrs. Montague in dressing, and by the time she was ready to descend her good humor was thoroughly restored, for she certainly was a most regal looking woman in her elegant and becoming toilet.

"I do not believe there will be another dress here this evening as beautiful as this," Mona remarked, as she fastened the last fold in place, her pretty face flushing with genuine admiration for the artistic costume.

"It *is* handsome, and I look passably young in it, too; how old should you take me to be Ruth?" Mrs. Montague asked, with a smiling glance at her own reflection in the mirror.

"A trifle over thirty, perhaps," Mona replied, and the little exultant laugh which broke from her companion told her that she felt highly flattered by that estimate of her years.

"There!" she remarked, as she drew on her gloves, "you need do nothing more for me; go now and get ready yourself, or you will miss the opening promenade."

Mona hastened away to her own room, where she had everything laid out in the most orderly manner, ready to put on, and if Mrs. Montague could have seen the dainty undergarments and skirts spread upon her bed; the costly kid boots and silken hose for her pretty feet, she might have arched her eyebrows more than ever over the extravagant taste of her seamstress.

Mona arranged her hair with great care, as she had worn it on the evening when she attended the opera with Ray, and this done she was soon ready.

She looked lovely. The black net, with its dainty white trimmings, was very becoming to her delicate complexion. The lining to the corsage had been cut low, and her pure white neck gleamed like marble through the meshes of the dusky lace. There was no lining, either, to her sleeves and her beautifully rounded arms looked like bits of exquisite sculpture. She had turned the lace away in the shape of a V at her throat, and now finished it by pinning to her corsage the cluster of white violets which she had purchased in the morning.

She regretted that she had no gloves with her suitable for the occasion, but since she was only to sit in the balcony, she thought it would not matter much if she wore none, and her small white hands, with their rose-tinted finger-tips, were by no means unsightly objects.

She was very happy and light-hearted, as she turned for one last look in her mirror before leaving her room.

She smiled involuntarily at her own loveliness, and gave a gay little nod at the charming reflection as she turned away.

Then she went out and softly down a back stair-way to avoid the crowds of people who were going up and down the front way.

But, on reaching the lower floor, she was obliged to cross the main hall and drawing-room in order to reach the pavilion, which Mr. Wellington had caused to be erected outside on the lawn for dancing, and which was connected with the house by a covered passage leading from one of the long windows of the drawing-room.

Mona stood in the doorway a moment, feeling slightly embarrassed at the thought of going unattended to search for her seat in the balcony.

Just then a round, white arm was slipped about her waist, and a gay, girlish voice cried in her ear:

"Oh, Miss Richards! how perfectly lovely you look! Are you coming to the ball?"

Mona turned and smiled into the bright face of Kitty McKenzie, who was radiant in pink silk and white tulle.

"No, only as a spectator," she replied, with an answering smile. "Mr. Wellington has kindly offered me a seat in the balcony, where I shall enjoy watching the merrymakers."

"But do you not *like* to dance yourself?" questioned the girl.

"Oh, yes, indeed. I used to enjoy it very much," Mona replied, with a little sigh.

"Then I think it is a great pity that you cannot join us to-night," returned Miss Kitty, regretfully, for she had caught the sigh; "only," she added, with sudden thought, "being in mourning, perhaps you would rather not."

"No, I should not care to dance to-night," Mona returned, and then she became conscious that a familiar form was approaching the spot where they stood.

It was not an easy matter for her to keep back her color as Ray drew near, and try to appear as if she had never seen him before. She knew that he was choosing this opportunity

Mrs. Georgie Sheldon

to be formally introduced to her.

But the voluble Miss McKenzie saluted him in her frank outspoken manner.

"Oh, Mr. Palmer," she cried, "are not the rooms lovely?—the flowers, the lights, indeed *all* the decorations?"

"They are, truly, Miss McKenzie; and," he added, with a merry smile, as he glanced at her bright face and figure, and then turned his gaze upon Mona, "there are some other lovely adornments about the rooms, besides those so skillfully used by the professional decorator."

"Thank you—of course that was intended as a compliment to ourselves," the quick-witted little lady returned, as she dropped him a coquettish courtesy; "and," turning to Mona, "perhaps you would like an introduction to my friend. Miss Richards, allow me to present you to Mr. Palmer."

Ray bowed low over the white hand which Mona mechanically offered him, and which he clasped in a way to send a thrill leaping along her nerves that made the violets upon her bosom quiver, as if a breath of wind had swept over them.

She barely had time to acknowledge the presentation, however, when an icy voice behind her remarked:

"Miss Richards, Mr. Wellington is looking for you to conduct you to your seat in the balcony."

Turning, Mona saw Mrs. Montague regarding her with a look of cold displeasure, and she knew that she must have witnessed her introduction to Ray, and disapproved of it.

But she was secretly glad that she had been so near, for now she could feel free to recognize her lover whenever they met, without the fear of being questioned as to how she happened to know him.

"Mr. Wellington looking for Miss Richards, did you say, Mrs. Montague?" Ray inquired, quickly improving his opportunity, and looking about him in search of that gentleman. "Ah! I see him yonder—Miss Richards, allow me to conduct you to him."

He offered his arm in a ceremonious way, as any new acquaintance might have done, and led her slowly toward the spot where Mr. Wellington was standing, while Mrs. Montague watched them, with a frown upon her brow.

"I believe I was a fool to allow her to come down; she is far too pretty to appear in public with me; any one would suppose her to be an equal," she muttered, irritably. "Who would have believed," she added, "that she could have gotten herself up in that bewitching style, with only a few bits of white ribbon and not a single ornament! I wonder where she got her violets? She has exquisite taste, anyhow."

But Ray and Mona were unconscious of these jealous remarks. They were oblivious of everything just then, except the presence of each other and the fortunate circumstances which had thrown them together.

"My darling," Ray said, under his breath, "that was very cleverly managed, was it not? Don't you think I am quite a tactician? I caught sight of you the moment you appeared; then that bright fairy, Kitty McKenzie, arrived upon the scene, and I knew that my opportunity had come."

"But you almost took my breath away, Ray, when you bore me off so unceremoniously before Mrs. Montague's disapproving eyes," Mona murmured in response.

"Unceremonious!" the young man retorted, with assumed surprise, and a roguish smile. "Why, I thought I was excessively formal."

"Yes, in your manner to me; but you did not ask the lady's permission to conduct me to the host."

"How was I supposed to know that Miss Richards, to whom I had just been introduced, was not a guest as well as the more gorgeous, but less lovely, Mrs. Montague?" questioned the young lover, lightly. "But," he continued, with a sigh, "I cannot bear this sort of thing a great while. When I see you looking like some beautiful young goddess, I find it very difficult to assume an indifferent exterior. I nearly forgot myself a moment ago."

"Perhaps it would have been better if I had remained quietly in my own room," Mona archly returned, as she gave him a mischievous glance out of her bright eyes.

He drew the hand that lay on his arm close to his side with a fond pressure.

"Indeed, no!" he said, tenderly; "it is better to meet you thus than not at all. But must I give you up to Mr. Wellington?" he continued, in a wistful tone, as they drew near the gentleman. "No; I will ask him to direct me to the balcony, and I will conduct you there myself."

"Ah, Miss Richards, I have been looking for you," Mr. Wellington remarked, as his eye fell upon the fair girl. "It is almost time for the opening promenade, and you ought to be in your seat, so as not to miss anything. But wait a moment; I must speak to this gentleman first," he concluded, as some one approached him.

"Pray, Mr. Wellington, since you are so engaged, let me conduct Miss Richards to the balcony," Ray here interposed, as if the thought had just occurred to him.

Mr. Wellington, with a look of relief, readily assented to the proposition, and Ray and his companion were thus permitted to enjoy a little more of each other's society.

They easily found their way to the balcony, where Ray secured a good position for his *fiancee*.

"I suppose I will have to leave you now," he whispered in her ear; "I am engaged to Miss Wellington for the promenade; but, by and by, Mona, I shall steal away and come to you again."

"Do not leave the dancing on my account, Ray," Mona pleaded; "it is all so bright and lovely down there. I know you will enjoy it."

"I should, if I could have you with me," he interrupted, fondly; "but, as I cannot, I would much prefer to remain quietly here with you—only that would not do, I suppose."

"No, indeed," she returned, decidedly. "Now you *must* go, for the orchestra is beginning to play."

He left her, with a fond hand-clasp that brought a happy smile to her red lips, and went below to seek his host's daughter.

Mona was very glad, later on, that she was not below with the dancers, for she saw quite a number of people from New York, whom she knew, and she would not have cared to be recognized by them—or rather snubbed by them.

It was a brilliant scene when the grand procession formed.

The pavilion had been very tastefully decorated, and one would hardly have believed that there were only bare, rough boards behind the artistically draped damask silk and lace, which had been used in profusion to conceal them. The spacious room was brilliantly lighted; flowers and potted plants were everywhere, making the place bright with their varied hues, and sending forth their fragrance into every nook and corner, while the fine orchestra was concealed behind a screen of palms, mingled with oleanders in full bloom.

There must have been at least two hundred people present, the gentlemen, of course, in full evening dress, while the ladies' costumes were of exceeding richness and beauty, yet among them all, it is doubtful if there was one so happy as the lovely girl who sat so quietly in the balcony and watched the gay scene in which she could not mingle.

There were a good many people sitting there with her, and not a few regarded her with curious and admiring interest, and judged from her dress that she was in mourning, and that she was thus debarred, by the customs of society, from appearing in a ball-room as one of the dancers. That she was a lady no one doubted for a moment, for her every look and movement betrayed it.

Now and then Ray's fond glances would seek her, and, catching her eye, a little nod or smile plainly told her how he longed to be with her.

Mona saw Mrs. Montague conspicuous among the dancers, and she appeared to enter into the spirit of the occasion with almost the zest of a young girl during her first season; while it was noticed that Mr. Palmer was her companion more frequently than any other person.

She had come in with him for the grand march, and when the procession for supper was formed she was again upon his arm.

But Mona could not see Ray anywhere among this crowd, and the occupants of the balcony also going below for refreshment, she found herself almost alone in the pavilion.

But it was not for long, for presently she caught the sound of a quick, elastic step, and the next moment her lover was beside her.

"Come back a little, dear, where we can sit in the shadow of the draperies, and we will have a precious half-hour all by ourselves," he said, in a low tone; "then in a few moments a servant will bring us up some supper."

"How thoughtful you are, Ray! But, truly, I do not care for anything to eat," Mona returned, as she arose and followed him to a cozy nook, where the draperies would partially conceal them from observation.

"I do, my brown-eyed lassie," Ray responded, emphatically; "after the violent exercise of the last two hours I am quite sure my inner man needs replenishing. Ah, James, you're a good fellow," he continued, as a tan-colored son of the South now made his appearance, bearing a tray of tempting viands. "Here, take this and drink my health by and by; but come back and get your tray in the course of half an hour."

The darky showed two rows of brilliant teeth as Ray slipped a silver dollar into his hand; then with a cheerful "Yes, sir—

thank'ee, sir," and a low bow he disappeared as suddenly as he had come.

Mona was hungry, in spite of her assertion to the contrary, and she enjoyed the rich treat that Ray had so thoughtfully provided for her, while he was full of fun and gayety, and they had a merry time up there all by themselves.

When the dancers began to return, Ray quietly remarked:

"My darling, I am not going down to the company again; I feel guilty to have you sit moping here, while I am playing the gallant cavalier to other girls."

Mona laughed out softly, but gleefully, at this speech.

"I trust you will always be as conscientious and dutiful, my loyal knight," she roguishly retorted.

"You will never have cause to question my loyalty, my own," he whispered, with a look that brought a bright color into her cheeks.

"But I have not been moping," Mona resumed. "I have enjoyed being here and watching the dancers very much, and you know I could not join them even if my present position did not debar me," she tremulously concluded.

"True; I had not thought of that," the young man said, gravely, as his eye swept over her black dress.

"So, then, if you feel that your duty is below, do not hesitate about leaving me," Mona urged.

"I am not going," he firmly reiterated. "I have been formally introduced to 'Miss Richards,' and I have a perfect right to cultivate her acquaintance if I choose."

Mona did not urge him further; she saw that he really wished to stay, and she was only too happy to have him there by her side; and so the lovers passed two delightful hours, watching the gay throng below, now and then exchanging fond looks or a few low spoken words, and only one pair of eyes among the multitude espied and recognized them.

These belonged to Louis Hamblin, whose eyes lighted with sudden triumph, while an evil smile played over his face as he saw them.

"I thought so," he muttered, as he noticed Ray Palmer's attitude of devotion. "That would prove the truth of my suspicions, if nothing else did so."

CHAPTER XXIII

LOUIS HAMBLIN IS JEALOUS OF RAY

It was after one o'clock when Mona told Ray that she must go to her room, so as to be in readiness to assist Mrs. Montague when she came up from the pavilion.

Ray was loath to let her go; he longed to keep her there with him until the last moment, but he felt that she was the best judge of her duty, and he would not interfere with it, since he had conceded the point of her remaining with Mrs. Montague for the present.

He arose to accompany her through the pavilion and drawing-room to the hall.

"Will it not be better for me to go alone?" asked Mona, fearing that she might be made conspicuous by this attention.

"Through all that crowd!" exclaimed her lover, surprised. "No, indeed; I would not allow any lady whom I knew to go unattended, and since it is known that I have been formally presented to Miss Richards, why should I not treat her with becoming politeness?"

Mona made no further objection, but quietly took his arm

and allowed him to have his way. She was proud and happy to know that Ray was noble-minded enough to have no fear of being seen publicly showing courtesy to a simple seamstress.

As they were passing through the drawing-room Mona caught sight of Mrs. Montague and Mr. Palmer sitting in an alcove by themselves.

Both glanced up, for the young couple were obliged to pass near them, and Mrs. Montague frowned as she saw her waiting-maid, for the second time that evening, upon the arm of Ray.

Mr. Palmer flushed and appeared somewhat embarrassed as he met his son's eye, although he nodded and smiled in his usual genial way.

Reaching the main hall, Ray led Mona to the foot of the stairs, and held out his hand for a parting clasp.

"Good-night, my darling," he said, bending over her and speaking in a low tone. "Do you know that you are all the world to me, and I shall impatiently count the days until I can claim you—three months hence at the farthest! I must say good-by, too," he added, "as we leave for New York early in the morning; but I shall try to see you again in a few days."

Mona smiled, a delicate flush suffusing her face at his fond words; then, responding to his good-night, she went quickly up stairs and sought her room, firmly believing that she was the happiest person at Hazeldean, and that her lover was the noblest man in the world.

Louis Hamblin had seen the young couple leave the pavilion,

and following them at a distance, had watched them with a jealous eye as they took leave of each other.

Another pair of eyes were also peering at them over the banister in the upper hall, and a beautiful face clouded over with anger and jealousy when Ray bent, with that earnest, luminous look, to whisper his parting in Mona's ear.

They belonged to a brilliant society belle, Miss Josephine Holt, who had long entertained a secret affection for Ray.

She also knew Mona, having met her in society earlier in the season, and had been jealous of the young man's attentions to her.

She wondered at finding her there at Hazeldean, for she knew of her loss of fortune. She slipped out of sight into a dressing-room as Mona came up stairs, and, finding Miss Merrill there, asked her, in an indifferent tone, as Mona passed the door, who the young lady was.

"Oh, that is Ruth Richards—Mrs. Montague's waiting-maid," was the reply.

A smile of scorn leaped to Miss Holt's proud lips as she heard the name.

"Ruth Richards," she repeated to herself. "So this is how she disappeared so suddenly out of the knowledge of everybody. A common waiting-maid, and too proud to sail under her own name! I wonder if she is a relative of Mrs. Montague? If she is, perhaps that lady objected to having it known, and so called her Ruth Richards. Can it be possible that Ray Palmer is attentive to her *now*? Does he know that she is sailing under false colors? I think I will look into this state of affairs a little!"

The young lady donned her wraps and took her departure from Hazeldean, but with an angry frown upon her brow, for her enjoyments of the evening had been entirely spoiled by the little scene which she had just witnessed.

After Ray left Mona he drew his outside coat on over his evening dress and went out into the grounds for a quiet smoke and to think, for he felt troubled and nervous.

His father's flush and embarrassment, as he caught his eye while passing through the drawing-room, were a revelation to him.

Mona had spoken to him of his attentions to Mrs. Montague, and he had also observed them, since coming to Hazeldean, but he had hoped that they were only temporary, and would not amount to anything serious.

But to-night it was only too evident that the beautiful and dashing widow had acquired a strong influence over his father, and he began to fear that he was seriously contemplating making her his wife.

He was startled and shocked—not because of any unreasonable jealousy, or a selfish aversion to the thought of having his father take a congenial companion into his home; but he feared she was not a woman to make him happy. She was gay and worldly; she lived for and in the excitement of society, while Mr. Palmer was more quiet and domestic in his tastes.

Besides, he had somehow became imbued with the idea that she was lacking in principle. Perhaps what Mona had told him about her, in connection with her mother's history, might have given him this impression; but, whatever had caused it, he shrank with the greatest repugnance from having her

Mrs. Georgie Sheldon

become the wife of his father.

Still he felt helpless to prevent it; he experienced great delicacy about making any objections if his father should intimate a wish to change his condition, and he could readily see that by so doing he would not only deeply wound him, but be likely to make an enemy of Mrs. Montague.

So these were the things he wished to think over by himself, and that sent him out into the grounds after he had left Mona.

The night was a beautiful one. There was not a cloud in the sky, and the full moon was sailing in matchless majesty through the star-studded vault above, while the brilliantly lighted house and park, with the entrancing music from the pavilion floating out to him on the still air, added their charm to the scene.

Ray lighted his cigar and strolled down the avenue, his heart filled with conflicting emotions. He was very happy in his new relations with Mona, yet strangely uneasy and depressed regarding his father's prospects.

There was a line of great Norway spruce trees along one side of the avenue, not far from the main road, and as Ray, deeply absorbed in his own thoughts, was passing these, a figure suddenly stepped out from among them and accosted him.

It was Louis Hamblin.

"Ah, Palmer," he said, affably, "out for a smoke? Give me a light, will you?"

"Certainly," Ray responded, cordially, and politely extended his cigar to him.

The man made use of it, then returned it, with thanks, remarking, as he turned to walk along with him:

"Glorious night, this!"

"Indeed it is—we seldom have so perfect an evening," Ray heartily responded.

"Quite a blow-out, too," added Mr. Hamblin, who was somewhat given to slang. "Wellington is a generous old codger, and has done things up in fine style."

"Yes, I should say the ball has been a great success, at least everybody has appeared to enjoy it," Ray politely replied.

He was not very well pleased with the young man's enforced companionship; he would have much preferred to be left to his own reflections.

"That is so, and there were lots of pretty girls on the floor," Mr. Hamblin went on, in his free-and-easy style, "and the costumes were exceptionally fine, too. By the way," with a covert look at Ray, "that Miss Montague is a remarkably beautiful girl."

Ray felt a great inward shock go through him at this observation, and he was on his guard in an instant.

"Miss Montague!" he repeated, bending a keen glance upon his companion, "was there a *Miss* Montague here this evening?"

"I beg ten thousand pardons, Palmer," the young man broke forth, with well-assumed confusion, "I don't know why I used that name, 'pon my word I don't, unless it was because of association. I'd heard, you know, that you were attentive at one time to a Miss Montague, niece to that rich old chap, Dinsmore, who died recently. The name I should have spoken, however, was Miss Richards, with whom I saw you talking a while ago."

Louis Hamblin had at once suspected Mona's identity, upon discovering the lovers sitting together in the balcony. He was confirmed in this suspicion when he followed them from the pavilion and observed their tender parting in the hall, and so he had dogged Ray's steps, when he went out for a walk, with the express purpose of pumping him, and had thus tried to take him off his guard by speaking of Mona in the way he did.

"Ah, yes," Ray quietly responded, for he had seen through the trick at once; "Miss Kitty McKenzie introduced me to Miss Richards early in the evening. She is an interesting girl, and she informs me that she is in the employ of your aunt, Mrs. Montague."

"Yes, she's seamstress, or something of that sort," Mr. Hamblin returned, knocking the ashes from his cigar. "Deuced shame, isn't it, that a pretty, lady-like girl like her should have to work at such a trade for her living? I—I believe," with a sly glance at Ray, "if I wasn't dependent on Aunt Margie—that is, if I had a fortune of my own—I'd like nothing better than to marry the girl and put her in a position more befitting her beauty."

It was fortunate, for Mona's sake, that they were walking in the shadow of the tall spruces, or Louis Hamblin must have seen the look of wrath that kindled on Ray's face at the presumptuous speech.

His first impulse was to hurl the conceited puppy to the ground for daring to speak of his betrothed in that flippant manner; but such a demonstration he knew would involve serious consequences, and at once betray Mona's identity and make it impossible for her to learn anything from Mrs. Montague regarding her mother's history.

He had a terrible struggle within himself for a moment before he could control his anger sufficiently to make any reply. But after two or three vigorous puffs at his Havana, he managed to say, with some degree of calmness, though with an undertone of sarcasm, which he could not restrain, and which did not fail to make itself felt:

"Really, Hamblin, your philanthropic spirit is a great credit to you, and doubtless Miss Richards would appreciate it if she could know of your deep interest in her. But, if I am not mistaken, I have heard that you are contemplating matrimony in another quarter—that Miss McKenzie is the bright, particular star in your firmament; and she is really a charming young lady in my estimation."

"Oh, Kitty is well enough," returned Mr. Hamblin, with a shrug of his shoulders, "but a fellow doesn't quite relish having a girl thrust upon him. Aunt Marg is set upon my marrying her, and it's human nature, you know, never to want to do anything under compulsion, but to be inclined to do just what you know you must not. Eh, Palmer?"

What could the fellow mean? Ray asked himself. Did he still suspect, in spite of his efforts to conceal the fact, who Ruth Richards really was? And did he mean to imply, by his moralizing, that he knew how Ray longed to thrash him for his insolence, and yet knew he must not, for fear of compromising the girl he loved?

Then, too, he could not help despising him for the slighting and insulting way in which he had spoken of Kitty

McKenzie, who, he felt, was far too true and lovely a girl to throw herself away upon such a flippant and unprincipled fellow.

He knew that he could not tamely submit to much more conversation of such a nature, so he merely replied in an absent tone.

"Perhaps." Then tossing away his cigar, he added: "I believe I heard a clock strike two a few moments ago. I think I shall go in and retire, as I have important business to attend to in the morning."

"Sure enough! I heard something about the case of the diamond robbery coming off to-morrow," responded Mr. Hamblin, in an eager tone. "That was a queer affair throughout, wasn't it?—and the story about the Bently woman is another—it got into the papers in spite of all old Vanderheck's efforts to bribe the reporters to silence. Do you credit the theory that the same woman was concerned in both swindles?"

"I hardly know what to think about it," Ray answered. "We do not even know yet whether the cross belongs to us; but Mr. Rider is confident that Mrs. Bently, of the Chicago affair, and Mrs. Vanderbeck, or 'heck'—whatever her name may be—are one and the same person."

"Well, it is certain that Mrs. Vanderheck, of New York, who figures so conspicuously in society, has an enormous store of diamonds, however she came by them," Louis Hamblin remarked.

Then, having reached the house, Ray bade him a brief good-night, and went immediately up to his room.

He found his father there before him and walking up and down the floor in an unusually thoughtful mood.

"Ah, Ray!" he said, as his son entered, "I have been waiting for you. I want to have a little talk with you before we go to bed."

"About the examination of to-morrow?" Ray inquired, with a keen glance.

"No—about—Ray, how would you like it if I should—well, to out with it at once—if I should marry again?" and the embarrassed old gentleman grew crimson even to the bald spot upon his head, as he then blundered through his question.

Ray sat down before he allowed himself to reply.

Now that the crisis had really come, he found he had less strength to meet it than he had anticipated.

"Well, father," he gravely said, after a moment of thought, "if you think that a second marriage is essential to your comfort and happiness, I should not presume to oppose it."

Mr. Palmer bent an anxious look upon his son.

"And yet you do not exactly approve of the plan?" he observed.

Ray looked up and frankly met his father's eye.

He believed it would be better to speak his mind freely than to dissemble in any way.

"I cannot fail to understand your meaning, for, of course, I

Mrs. Georgie Sheldon

have not been blind of late," he remarked. "I have seen how agreeable the society of Mrs. Montague is to you, and, judging from appearances, yours is no less so to her. I am bound to confess that she is a very handsome woman and very charming also in company. Still it is plain to be seen that she is a thorough society woman, and the question in my mind is, would you, with your more quiet tastes and disposition, enjoy sharing the kind of life that she leads?"

"But—I think—I hope that she would enjoy quiet home life and—my companionship, more than society, after our marriage," Mr. Palmer remarked, with some confusion.

Ray smiled slightly, for he saw that his father was very far gone, and he doubted if any argument would convince him that the fascinating widow would not be satisfied to settle down to the quieter joys of domestic life, even after she had succeeded in capturing the wealthy diamond merchant.

Still he resolved that he would say all that he had to say now, and then leave the matter with him to decide as his heart and judgment dictated.

"I hope that you will not deceive yourself, father," he said. "Mrs. Montague's nature is one that craves excitement and admiration, and she has been so long accustomed to this kind of life I imagine it would be impossible for her to resign it, cheerfully, for any one. Of course I know but very little of her personally, and I do not wish to judge her unfairly; but I should be very sorry to have you take any step which you would be likely to hereafter regret."

Mr. Palmer looked grave. His judgment, his common sense told him that Ray was right; that the gay woman of the world would not be willing to sacrifice her pleasures to his wishes, would never meet the wants of his more quiet and home-loving nature.

But he had been blinded and captivated by Mrs. Montague's wiles and preference for his society; he had, in fact, been led on so far that he saw no way of maintaining his dignity and honor except by making her a formal offer of his hand.

"You have no personal objection to her, I hope, Ray," he said, without replying to his remarks. "I assure you," he added, "the change shall not affect your prospects in any way. I will make handsome settlements upon you, and turn over the business to you before I take any important step."

"Thank you, sir," Ray heartily responded, but realizing that the matter was as good as settled, and it would be useless to discuss it any further. "Of course I should not feel at liberty to oppose you, were I so inclined, in a matter which concerns you so exclusively; as I said before, if you feel that such an alliance will be for your comfort and happiness, I would not wish to lay any obstacle in your way."

"You are very good, my son," Mr. Palmer returned, and yet he felt far from comfortable over the very doubtful approbation of his choice.

He had made up his mind to marry Mrs. Montague; he had indeed been almost upon the point of offering himself to her, just as Ray and Mona had passed through the drawing-room, when he had suddenly resolved to wait and consult his son, before taking the irrevocable step. He felt that he owed it to him to do so, for they had been good friends and confidants for so many years.

"I must be looking out for number one, you know," he added, trying to speak playfully; "for you will be getting married yourself one of these days, and the old home would be very lonely without you."

Ray wondered, with a twinge of bitterness, if his father could have forgotten how often he had told him that he "could never bear to be separated from him, and that when he found a wife to suit him, he must bring her home to brighten up the house and help to take care of him."

Now, it was evident, from what he had just said, that he would be expected to make a home for himself and his bride elsewhere.

"I wish you could find the girl you love, Ray," he went on, wistfully, as he did not reply. "It is rather hard on you that she should have disappeared so unaccountably. By the way, who was that lovely maiden with you a while ago?"

"She was introduced to me as Miss Richards," Ray responded, evasively, and flushing slightly.

Mr. Palmer looked up, surprised.

"So it was!" he exclaimed; "but I did not recognize her; and yet I thought there was something familiar about her. I suppose it was because she was in evening dress. Well, she is a charming little girl, anyhow. I only hope your Mona is as pretty, and that you'll find her soon. But suppose we go to bed," he said, with a weary sigh; "I'm tired, and we must be off early to-morrow morning."

The conclusion of this story, and what fortunes befell Mona, are fully told in the sequel to this volume entitled "True Love's Reward."

Choose from Thousands of 1stWorldLibrary Classics By

A. M. Barnard	Booth Tarkington	Edward Everett Hale
Ada Leverson	Boyd Cable	Edward J. O'Biren
Adolphus William Ward	Bram Stoker	Edward S. Ellis
Aesop	C. Collodi	Edwin L. Arnold
Agatha Christie	C. E. Orr	Eleanor Atkins
Alexander Aaronsohn	C. M. Ingleby	Eleanor Hallowell Abbott
Alexander Kielland	Carolyn Wells	Eliot Gregory
Alexandre Dumas	Catherine Parr Traill	Elizabeth Gaskell
Alfred Gatty	Charles A. Eastman	Elizabeth McCracken
Alfred Ollivant	Charles Amory Beach	Elizabeth Von Arnim
Alice Duer Miller	Charles Dickens	Ellem Key
Alice Turner Curtis	Charles Dudley Warner	Emerson Hough
Alice Dunbar	Charles Farrar Browne	Emilie F. Carlen
Allen Chapman	Charles Ives	Emily Bronte
Alleyne Ireland	Charles Kingsley	Emily Dickinson
Ambrose Bierce	Charles Klein	Enid Bagnold
Amelia E. Barr	Charles Hanson Towne	Enilor Macartney Lane
Amory H. Bradford	Charles Lathrop Pack	Erasmus W. Jones
Andrew Lang	Charles Romyn Dake	Ernie Howard Pie
Andrew McFarland Davis	Charles Whibley	Ethel May Dell
Andy Adams	Charles Willing Beale	Ethel Turner
Angela Brazil	Charlotte M. Braeme	Ethel Watts Mumford
Anna Alice Chapin	Charlotte M. Yonge	Eugene Sue
Anna Sewell	Charlotte Perkins Stetson	Eugenie Foa
Annie Besant	Clair W. Hayes	Eugene Wood
Annie Hamilton Donnell	Clarence Day Jr.	Eustace Hale Ball
Annie Payson Call	Clarence E. Mulford	Evelyn Everett-green
Annie Roe Carr	Clemence Housman	Everard Cotes
Annonaymous	Confucius	F. H. Cheley
Anton Chekhov	Coningsby Dawson	F. J. Cross
Archibald Lee Fletcher	Cornelis DeWitt Wilcox	F. Marion Crawford
Arnold Bennett	Cyril Burleigh	Fannie E. Newberry
Arthur C. Benson	D. H. Lawrence	Federick Austin Ogg
Arthur Conan Doyle	Daniel Defoe	Ferdinand Ossendowski
Arthur M. Winfield	David Garnett	Fergus Hume
Arthur Ransome	Dinah Craik	Florence A. Kilpatrick
Arthur Schnitzler	Don Carlos Janes	Fremont B. Deering
Arthur Train	Donald Keyhoe	Francis Bacon
Atticus	Dorothy Kilner	Francis Darwin
B.H. Baden-Powell	Dougan Clark	Frances Hodgson Burnett
B. M. Bower	Douglas Fairbanks	Frances Parkinson Keyes
B. C. Chatterjee	E. Nesbit	Frank Gee Patchin
Baroness Emmuska Orczy	E. P. Roe	Frank Harris
Baroness Orczy	E. Phillips Oppenheim	Frank Jewett Mather
Basil King	E. S. Brooks	Frank L. Packard
Bayard Taylor	Earl Barnes	Frank V. Webster
Ben Macomber	Edgar Rice Burroughs	Frederic Stewart Isham
Bertha Muzzy Bower	Edith Van Dyne	Frederick Trevor Hill
Bjornstjerne Bjornson	Edith Wharton	Frederick Winslow Taylor

Friedrich Kerst
Friedrich Nietzsche
Fyodor Dostoyevsky
G.A. Henty
G.K. Chesterton
Gabrielle E. Jackson
Garrett P. Serviss
Gaston Leroux
George A. Warren
George Ade
Geroge Bernard Shaw
George Cary Eggleston
George Durston
George Ebers
George Eliot
George Gissing
George MacDonald
George Meredith
George Orwell
George Sylvester Viereck
George Tucker
George W. Cable
George Wharton James
Gertrude Atherton
Gordon Casserly
Grace E. King
Grace Gallatin
Grace Greenwood
Grant Allen
Guillermo A. Sherwell
Gulielma Zollinger
Gustav Flaubert
H. A. Cody
H. B. Irving
H. C. Bailey
H. G. Wells
H. H. Munro
H. Irving Hancock
H. R. Naylor
H. Rider Haggard
H. W. C. Davis
Haldeman Julius
Hall Caine
Hamilton Wright Mabie
Hans Christian Andersen
Harold Avery
Harold McGrath
Harriet Beecher Stowe
Harry Castlemon
Harry Coghill
Harry Houidini

Hayden Carruth
Helent Hunt Jackson
Helen Nicolay
Hendrik Conscience
Hendy David Thoreau
Henri Barbusse
Henrik Ibsen
Henry Adams
Henry Ford
Henry Frost
Henry James
Henry Jones Ford
Henry Seton Merriman
Henry W Longfellow
Herbert A. Giles
Herbert Carter
Herbert N. Casson
Herman Hesse
Hildegard G. Frey
Homer
Honore De Balzac
Horace B. Day
Horace Walpole
Horatio Alger Jr.
Howard Pyle
Howard R. Garis
Hugh Lofting
Hugh Walpole
Humphry Ward
Ian Maclaren
Inez Haynes Gillmore
Irving Bacheller
Isabel Cecilia Williams
Isabel Hornibrook
Israel Abrahams
Ivan Turgenev
J. G.Austin
J. Henri Fabre
J. M. Barrie
J. M. Walsh
J. Macdonald Oxley
J. R. Miller
J. S. Fletcher
J. S. Knowles
J. Storer Clouston
J. W. Duffield
Jack London
Jacob Abbott
James Allen
James Andrews
James Baldwin

James Branch Cabell
James DeMille
James Joyce
James Lane Allen
James Lane Allen
James Oliver Curwood
James Oppenheim
James Otis
James R. Driscoll
Jane Abbott
Jane Austen
Jane L. Stewart
Janet Aldridge
Jens Peter Jacobsen
Jerome K. Jerome
Jessie Graham Flower
John Buchan
John Burroughs
John Cournos
John F. Kennedy
John Gay
John Glasworthy
John Habberton
John Joy Bell
John Kendrick Bangs
John Milton
John Philip Sousa
John Taintor Foote
Jonas Lauritz Idemil Lie
Jonathan Swift
Joseph A. Altsheler
Joseph Carey
Joseph Conrad
Joseph E. Badger Jr
Joseph Hergesheimer
Joseph Jacobs
Jules Vernes
Julian Hawthrone
Julie A Lippmann
Justin Huntly McCarthy
Kakuzo Okakura
Karle Wilson Baker
Kate Chopin
Kenneth Grahame
Kenneth McGaffey
Kate Langley Bosher
Kate Langley Bosher
Katherine Cecil Thurston
Katherine Stokes
L. A. Abbot
L. T. Meade

L. Frank Baum
Latta Griswold
Laura Dent Crane
Laura Lee Hope
Laurence Housman
Lawrence Beasley
Leo Tolstoy
Leonid Andreyev
Lewis Carroll
Lewis Sperry Chafer
Lilian Bell
Lloyd Osbourne
Louis Hughes
Louis Joseph Vance
Louis Tracy
Louisa May Alcott
Lucy Fitch Perkins
Lucy Maud Montgomery
Luther Benson
Lydia Miller Middleton
Lyndon Orr
M. Corvus
M. H. Adams
Margaret E. Sangster
Margret Howth
Margaret Vandercook
Margaret W. Hungerford
Margret Penrose
Maria Edgeworth
Maria Thompson Daviess
Mariano Azuela
Marion Polk Angellotti
Mark Overton
Mark Twain
Mary Austin
Mary Catherine Crowley
Mary Cole
Mary Hastings Bradley
Mary Roberts Rinehart
Mary Rowlandson
M. Wollstonecraft Shelley
Maud Lindsay
Max Beerbohm
Myra Kelly
Nathaniel Hawthrone
Nicolo Machiavelli
O. F. Walton
Oscar Wilde

Owen Johnson
P.G. Wodehouse
Paul and Mabel Thorne
Paul G. Tomlinson
Paul Severing
Percy Brebner
Percy Keese Fitzhugh
Peter B. Kyne
Plato
Quincy Allen
R. Derby Holmes
R. L. Stevenson
R. S. Ball
Rabindranath Tagore
Rahul Alvares
Ralph Bonehill
Ralph Henry Barbour
Ralph Victor
Ralph Waldo Emmerson
Rene Descartes
Ray Cummings
Rex Beach
Rex E. Beach
Richard Harding Davis
Richard Jefferies
Richard Le Gallienne
Robert Barr
Robert Frost
Robert Gordon Anderson
Robert L. Drake
Robert Lansing
Robert Lynd
Robert Michael Ballantyne
Robert W. Chambers
Rosa Nouchette Carey
Rudyard Kipling
Saint Augustine
Samuel B. Allison
Samuel Hopkins Adams
Sarah Bernhardt
Sarah C. Hallowell
Selma Lagerlof
Sherwood Anderson
Sigmund Freud
Standish O'Grady
Stanley Weyman
Stella Benson
Stella M. Francis

Stephen Crane
Stewart Edward White
Stijn Streuvels
Swami Abhedananda
Swami Parmananda
T. S. Ackland
T. S. Arthur
The Princess Der Ling
Thomas A. Janvier
Thomas A Kempis
Thomas Anderton
Thomas Bailey Aldrich
Thomas Bulfinch
Thomas De Quincey
Thomas Dixon
Thomas H. Huxley
Thomas Hardy
Thomas More
Thornton W. Burgess
U. S. Grant
Upton Sinclair
Valentine Williams
Various Authors
Vaughan Kester
Victor Appleton
Victor G. Durham
Victoria Cross
Virginia Woolf
Wadsworth Camp
Walter Camp
Walter Scott
Washington Irving
Wilbur Lawton
Wilkie Collins
Willa Cather
Willard F. Baker
William Dean Howells
William le Queux
W. Makepeace Thackeray
William W. Walter
William Shakespeare
Winston Churchill
Yei Theodora Ozaki
Yogi Ramacharaka
Young E. Allison
Zane Grey